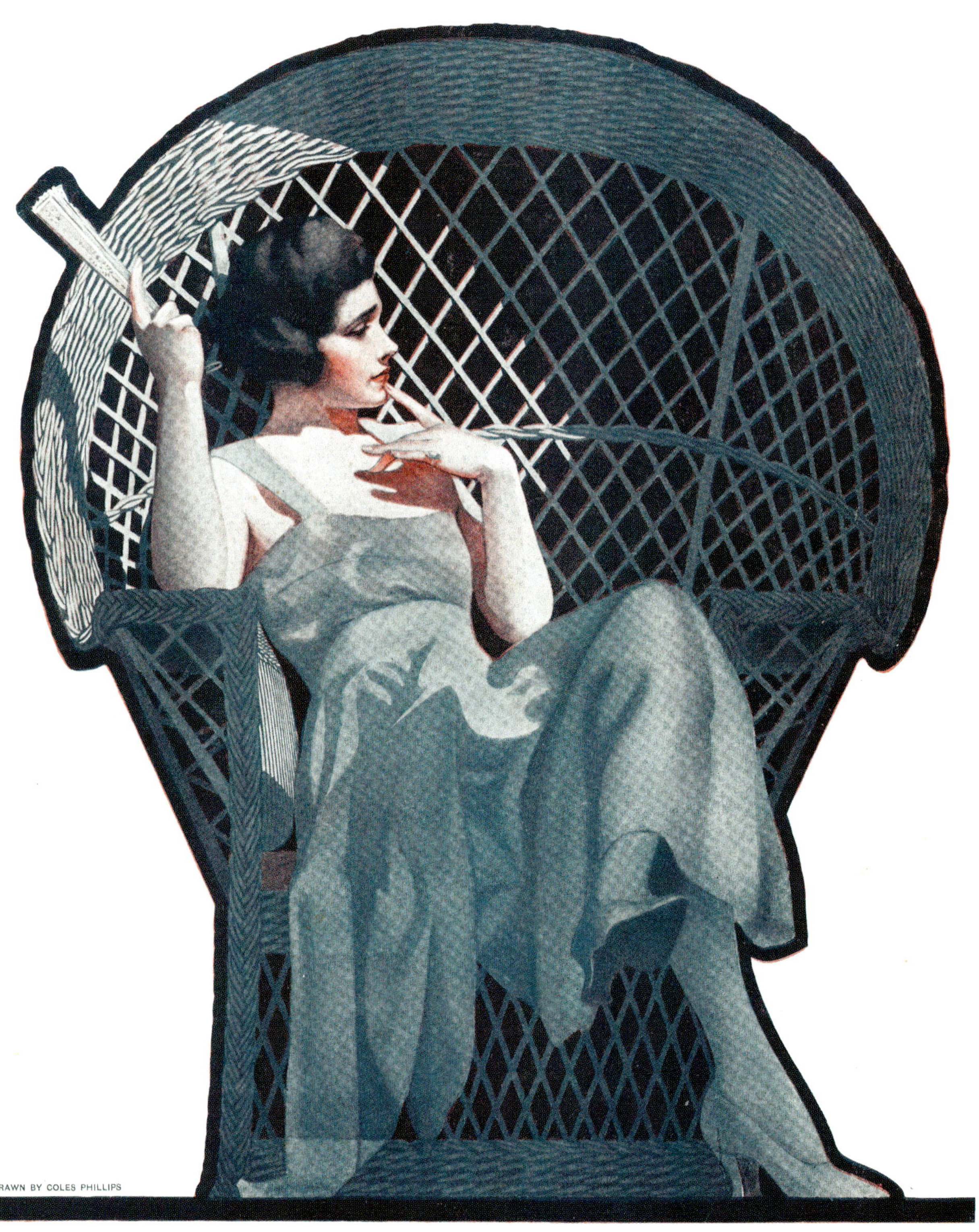

Cover art from *The Saturday Evening Post,* August 6, 1921

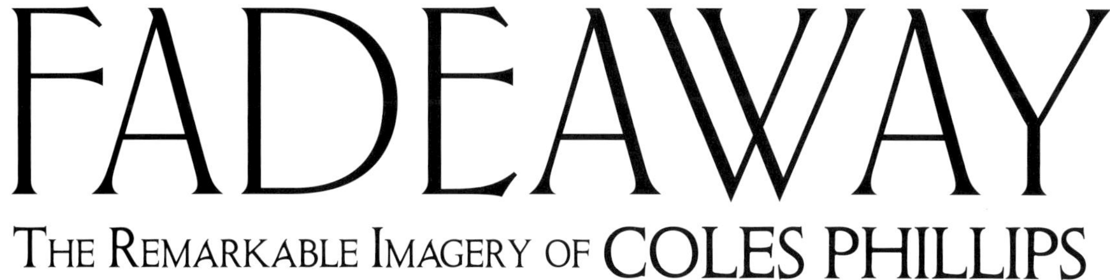

THE REMARKABLE IMAGERY OF COLES PHILLIPS

Edited by
Jeff A. Menges

Introduction by
Scott M. Fischer

DOVER PUBLICATIONS, INC.
Mineola, New York

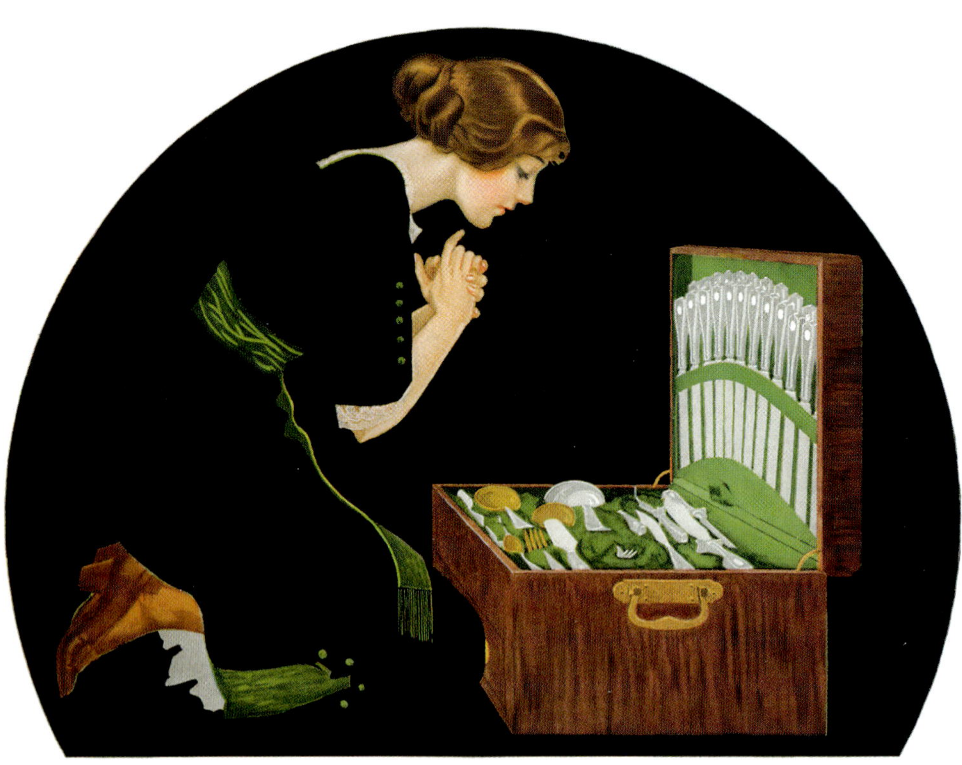

The Good Silver
Bobbs-Merrill Co., 1912

Copyright

Bibliographical Note

Fadeaway: The Remarkable Imagery of Coles Phillips, first published by Dover Publications, Inc., in 2019, is a new collection of illustrations by Coles Phillips, compiled by Jeff A. Menges from the following sources: *A Gallery of Girls* by Coles Phillips, originally published in 1911 by The Century Company, New York; *The Gorgeous Isle* by Gertrude Atherton, illustrated by Coles Phillips, originally published in 1908 by Doubleday, Page & Company, New York; and *A Young Man's Fancy* by Coles Phillips, originally published in 1912 by The Bobbs-Merrill Company, Indianapolis, Indiana. Additional plates were selected from various magazines from the early twentieth century. Scott M. Fischer has provided an Introduction for this work.

Library of Congress Cataloging-in-Publication Data

Names: Phillips, Coles, 1880–1927, artist. | Menges, Jeff A., editor. |
Fischer, Scott M., writer of introduction. | Phillips, Coles, 1880–1927.
Gallery of girls. Selections. | Phillips, Coles, 1880–1927. Young man's fancy. Selections.
Title: Fadeaway : the remarkable imagery of Coles Phillips / Coles Phillips ; edited by
Jeff A. Menges ; introduction by Scott M. Fischer.
Description: Mineola, New York : Dover Publications, 2019. | Series: Dover fine art,
history of art
Identifiers: LCCN 2018036642| ISBN 9780486828633 (paperback) | ISBN 0486828638
Subjects: LCSH: Phillips, Coles, 1880–1927—Themes, motives. | BISAC: ART /
Individual Artists / Monographs.
Classification: LCC NC975.5.P49 A4 2019 | DDC 741.6092—dc23
LC record available at https://lccn.loc.gov/2018036642

Manufactured in the United States by LSC Communications
82863801 2019
www.doverpublications.com

Contents

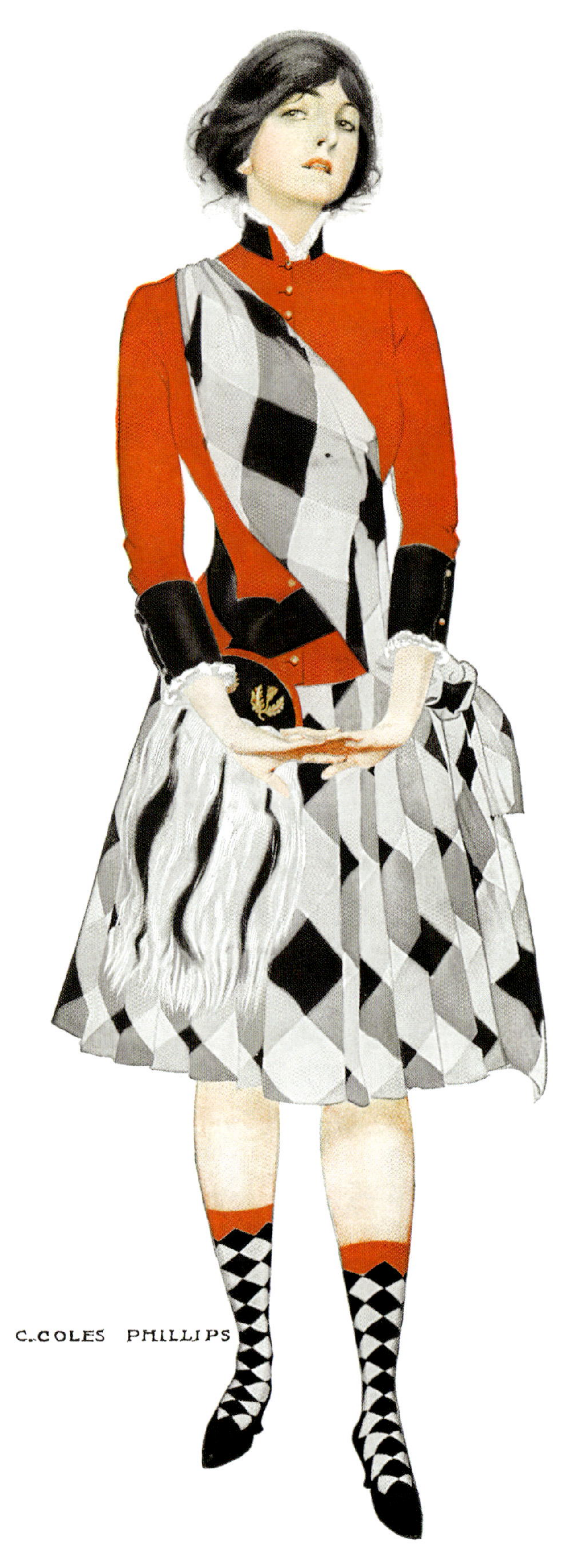

Hoot Mon!
Cover art from *Life* Magazine, October 20, 1910

Introduction

"Absence makes the heart grow fonder." While this phrase is not usually associated with art, in the case of illustrator Coles Phillips (1880–1927), it certainly applies.

In viewing Phillips's work, one is immediately struck by what *isn't* there. We quickly understand that what he chose *not* to paint is as important as what he chose to paint.

Myself, being an artist that is obsessed with the mechanics of great picture making, I might even argue that what Phillips left out of his paintings is actually more important than what he put into his paintings. Sure, an art director needs an illustration to have a subject by the very definition of the word "illustration." But today, some 100 years after Phillips was working, would we still be talking about him with the same reverence, if he had made the choice to paint every element in his work?

What I am looking for in great art is evidence that the artist was there, making bold decisions that often break the rules of reality. Because here is the thing—reality is a crutch. I am not suggesting that hyper-photorealistic art is easy. It requires amazing technique and a discipline that I do not possess. But what I am suggesting is that in this day and age of super HD imagery, you can always paint toward that observed perfection. If you want to render down to the pores on someone's nose you can; because the answers are in front of you the whole time.

I am much more interested in seeing an artist's *mind* at work. If they are a chunky painter, I want to see those brushstrokes taking us on the ride of an artist discovering the form of his subject. If they are a realistic painter I want to see where the artist deviated from that reality, and tiptoed into the surreal. If they are a portrait artist, I am looking for an unexpected moment in the pose or expression. And in the case of Coles Phillips, I revel in seeing his "math-mind" at work. For me, it isn't about how well Phillips rendered his subjects at all. Though he is an exceptional draftsman, there is no shortage of artists I can look at for painting technique. I am looking at him for the way he *saw* things more than the way he painted them.

My late twenties is when Coles Phillips started to have a serious impact on my art. Prior to that, my journey was all about technique. Once skill is acquired, though, the question becomes, "What do you want to do with it?" The old adage, "You have to learn the rules before you can break them," applies. And I wanted to break stuff. And what I began to realize was it did not matter how you frosted a cake, if the cake itself was as bland as cardboard. I don't care if you render like Chuck Close or Rembrandt, if you can't give me something unexpected, you've lost me. From that point on, I considered myself as much an editor as a painter. And few artists in history have the editing genius of Coles Philips.

To put this into context, we have to realize that Phillips was doing all of this long before Photoshop existed. But if you look at the work, though the subject matter is antiquated, it has a modern feel to it—as if you are seeing a Photoshop screen today. His mind is clearly working in layers. Like Photoshop, each element is on a layer, and he is deciding which layers to

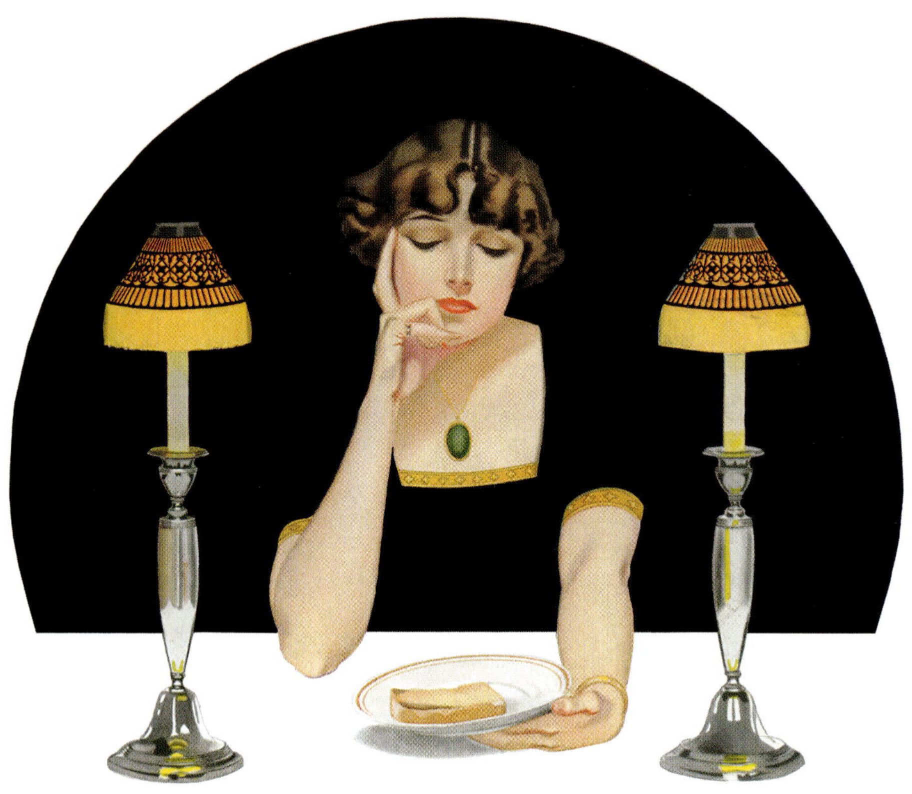

From *A Young Man's Fancy*
Bobbs-Merrill Co., 1912

turn on and off in his head in order to optically tease us. Just like a great puzzlemaker.

It is a bit of a paradox. In Phillips's "Fade Away" style, he is literally editing out elements (by making them the same flat color as the background), but those elements are still there. It is just that we, the viewer, are completing them with our mind. We are participating. To me the best works of art do this—allow for the viewer to participate in the process of completing the picture. I love it when you view a painting on the wall from 10 feet away and think it is a highly rendered subject, only to have it dissolve into brushstrokes upon closer examination. With Phillips, it is less about strokes and more about viewing ghosts of things that aren't there, but kind of are there. When everything is spelled out for us, art becomes less of a cooperative experience and more of a lecture.

To pull this off is no easy feat. There is little room for error. I am reminded of a quote by children's book illustrator Mo Willems, who said, "Simple and Easy are opposites." For Phillips, the results have a simplicity that is far from easy. One misplaced element and the entire image will fall apart. Your composition skills have to be off the charts, and beyond that, you have to be a master of "shape language." Pay attention to the silhouettes of his subjects. Phillips is a master of making sure the silhouette tells the story of his paintings, even if the silhouette is an implied silhouette. Because it shares the value/color of something behind it, we can read it.

There is an irony in the lasting affection artists have toward Coles Phillips. Probably because most artists want to be remembered for what they paint, and Coles Phillips is remembered for what he didn't.

Scott M. Fischer
July 2018

The Plates

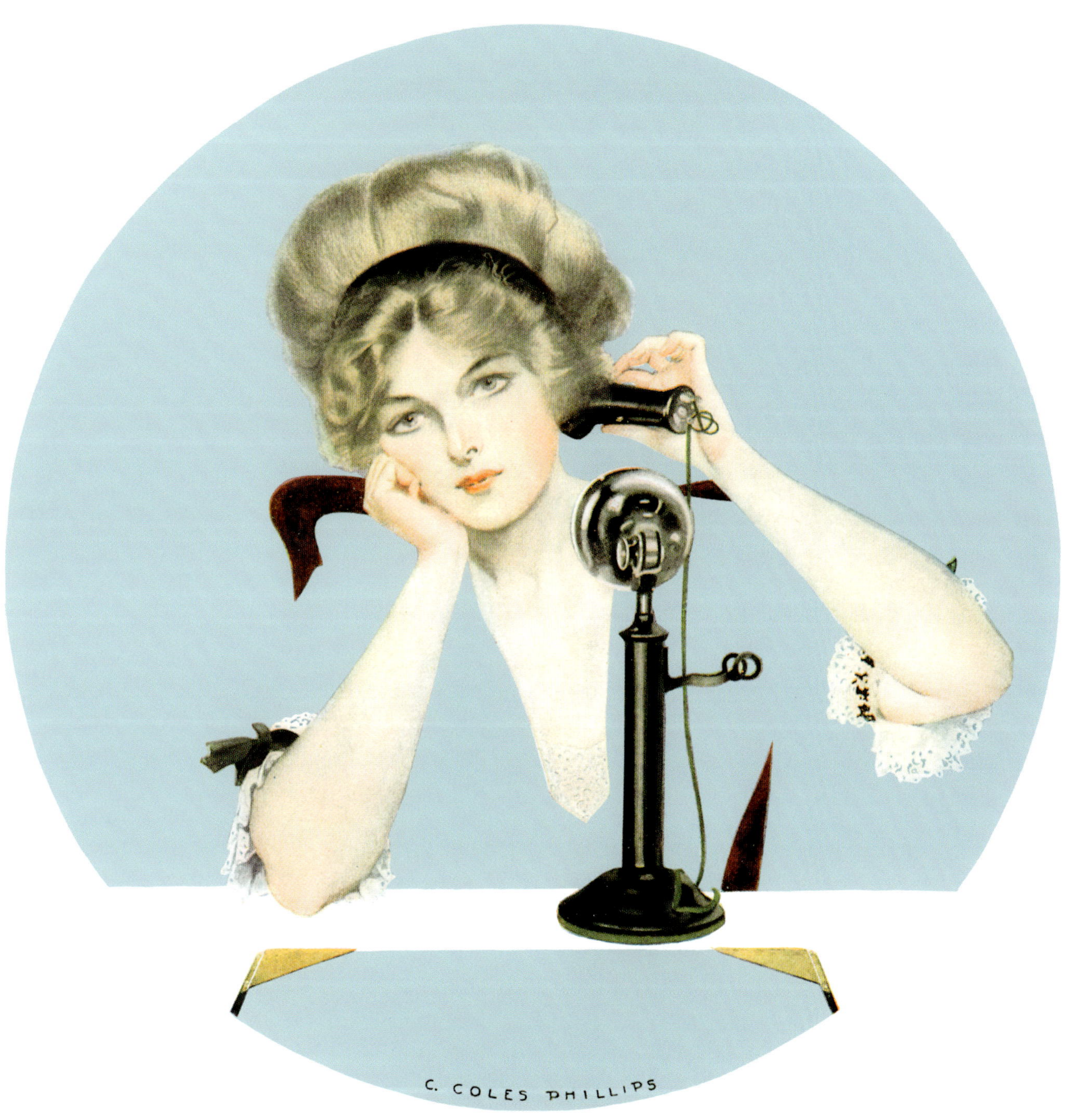

1. *Long Distance Lends Enchantment*
Cover art from *Life* Magazine, February 9, 1911

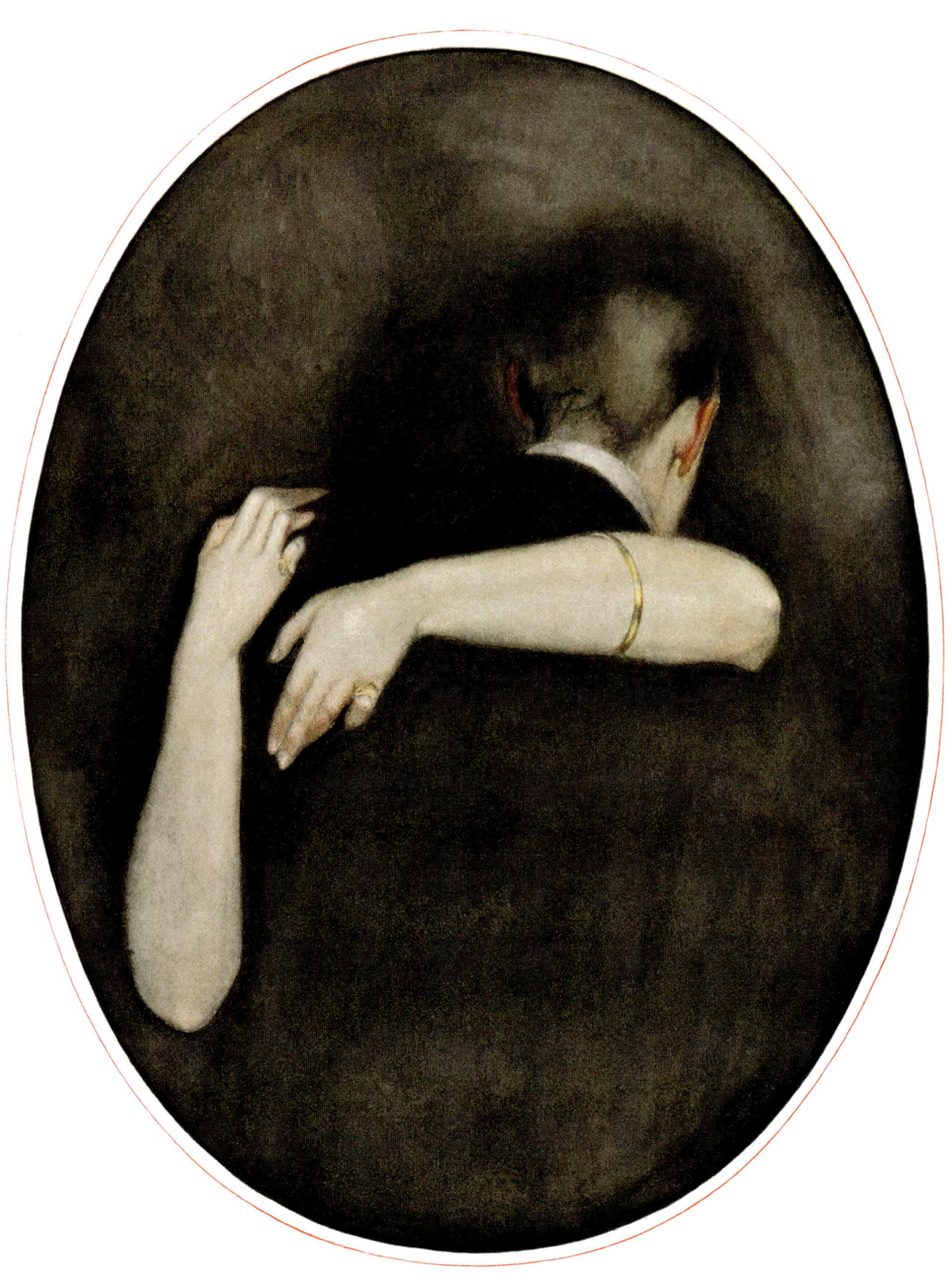

2. *Arms and the Man*
Cover art from *Life* Magazine, July 8, 1909

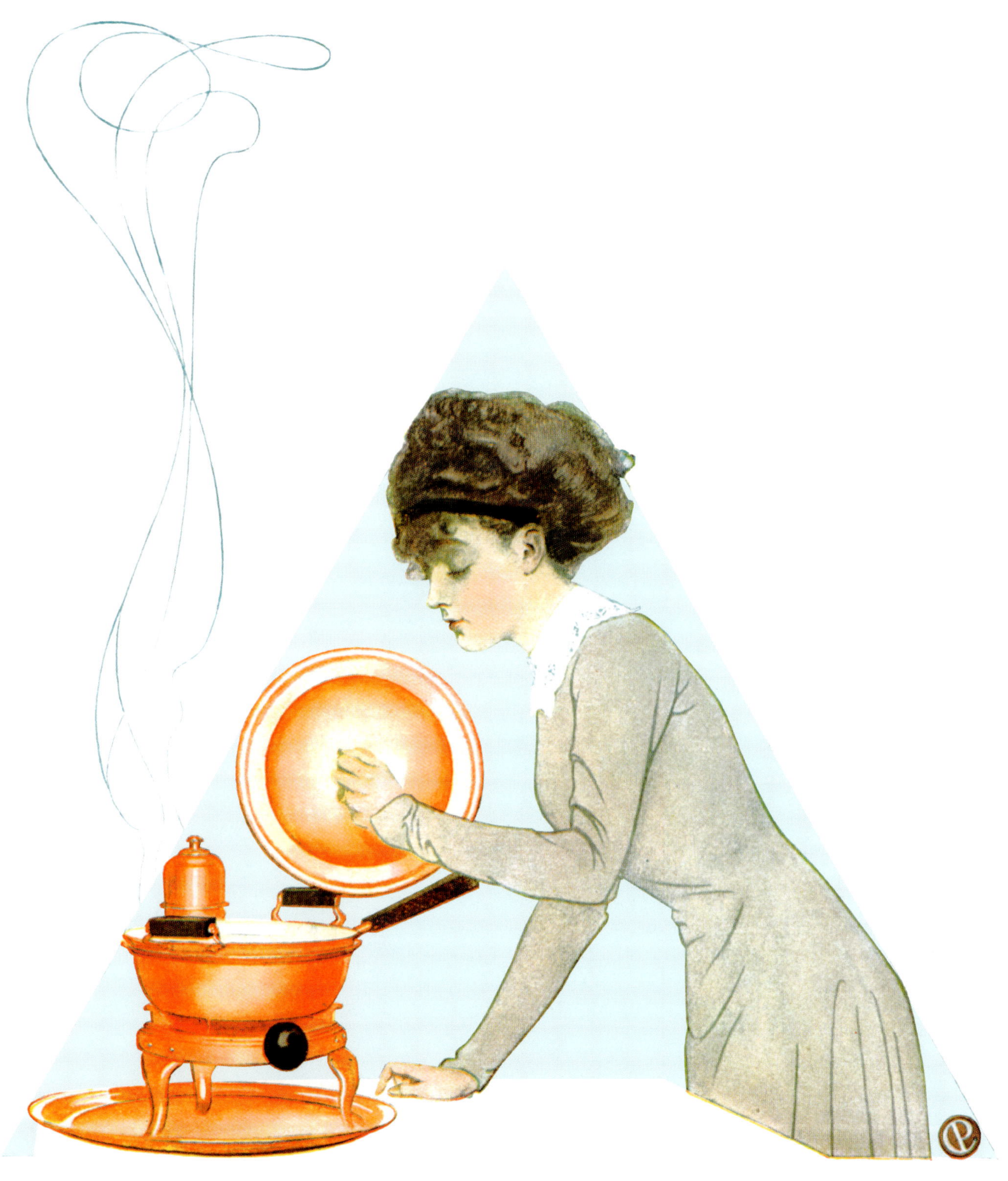

3. *Such Stuff as Dreams are Made On*
Cover art from *Life* Magazine, July 29, 1909

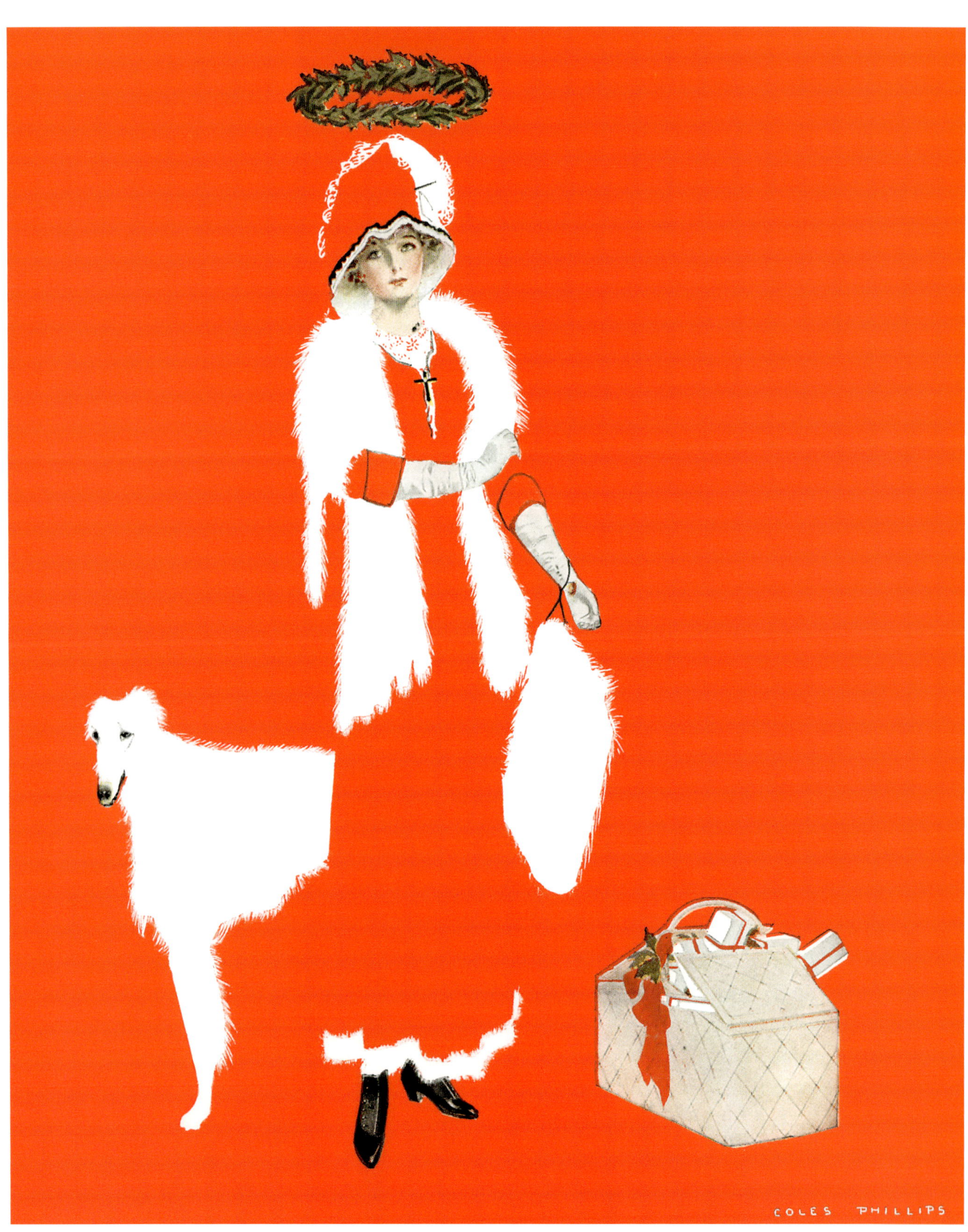

4. *A Present-Day Saint*
Cover art from *Life* Magazine, December 22, 1910

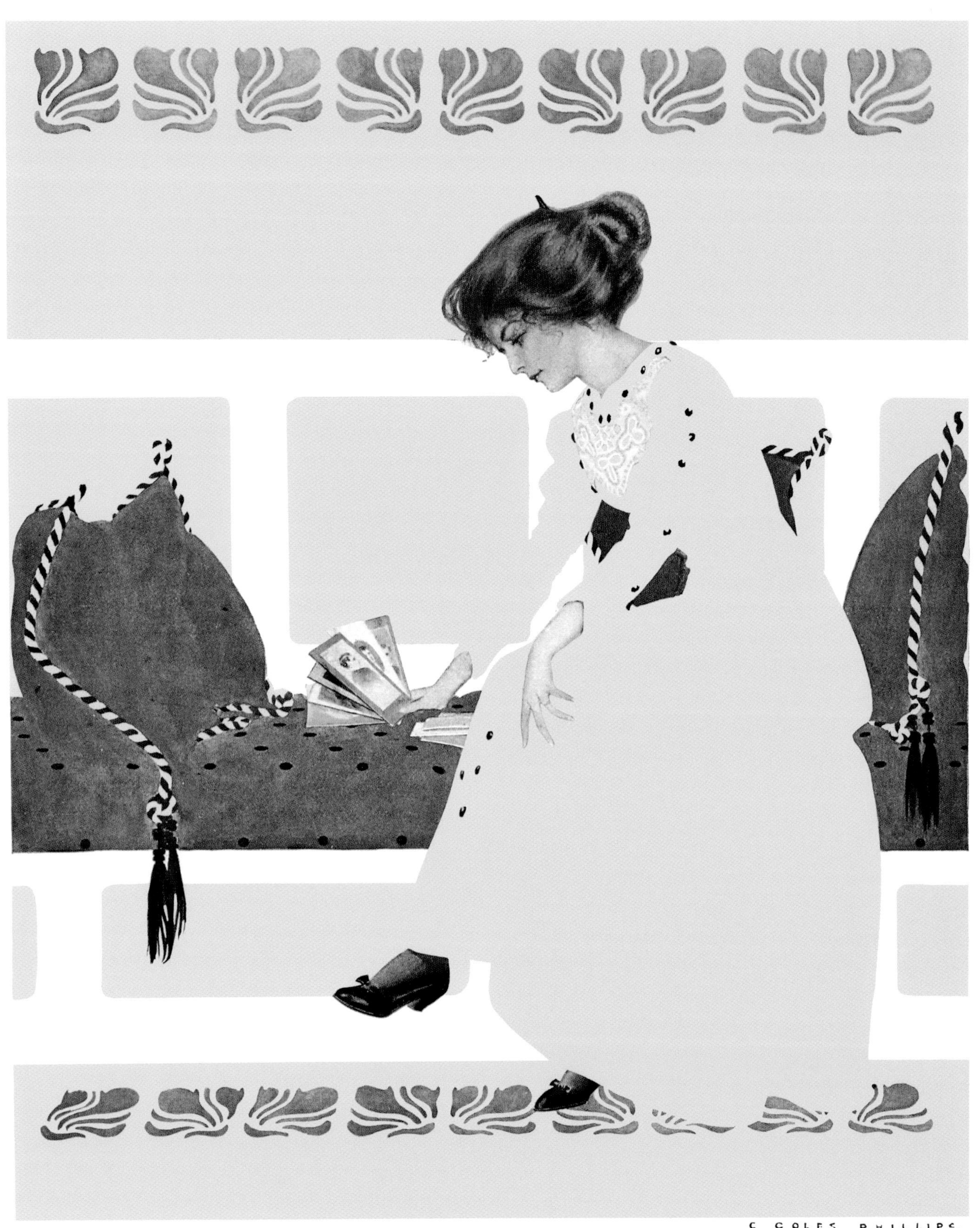

5. *Discarding from Strength*
Cover art from *Life* Magazine, May 12, 1910

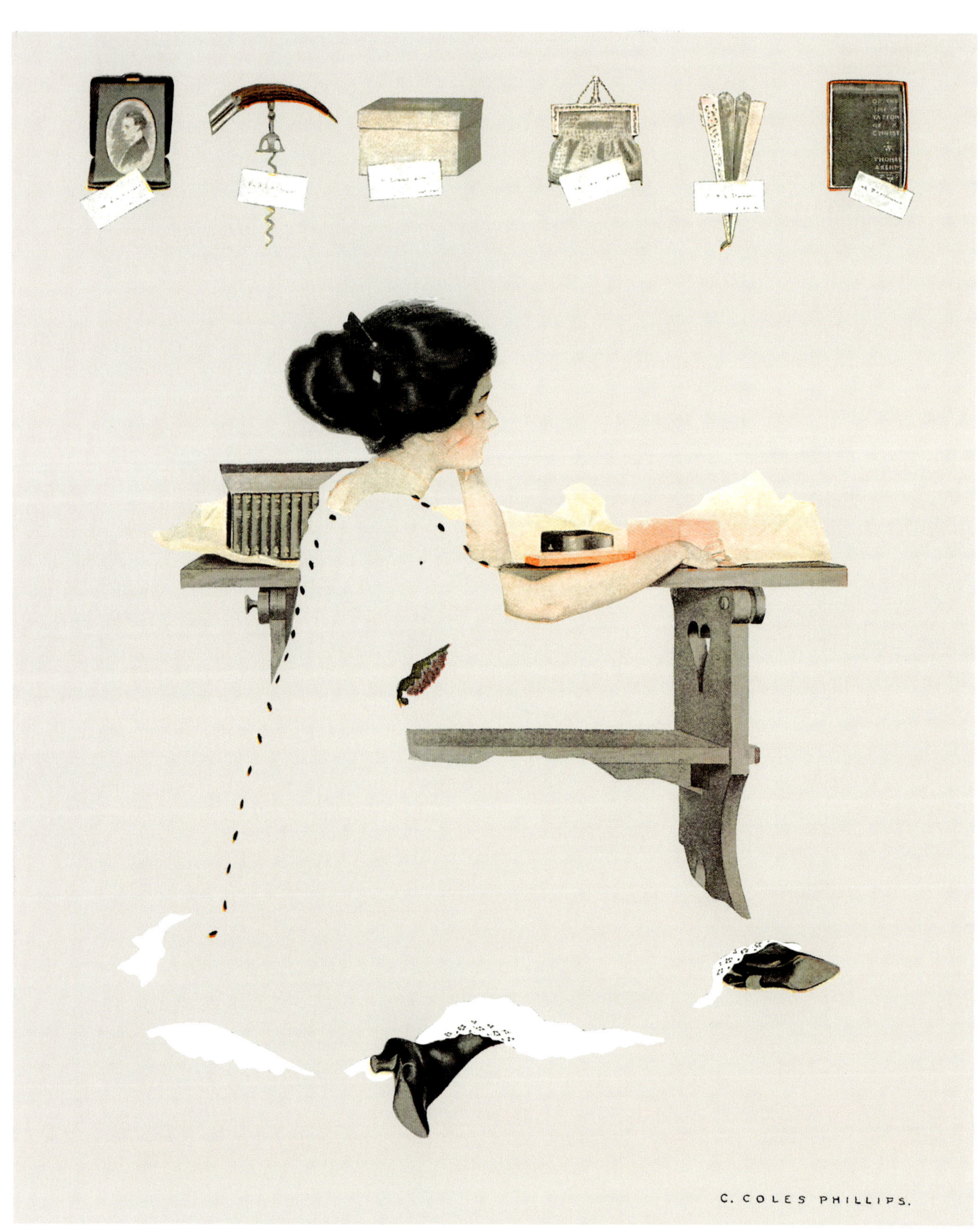

6. *Know All Men by These Presents*
Cover art from *Life* Magazine, January 27, 1910

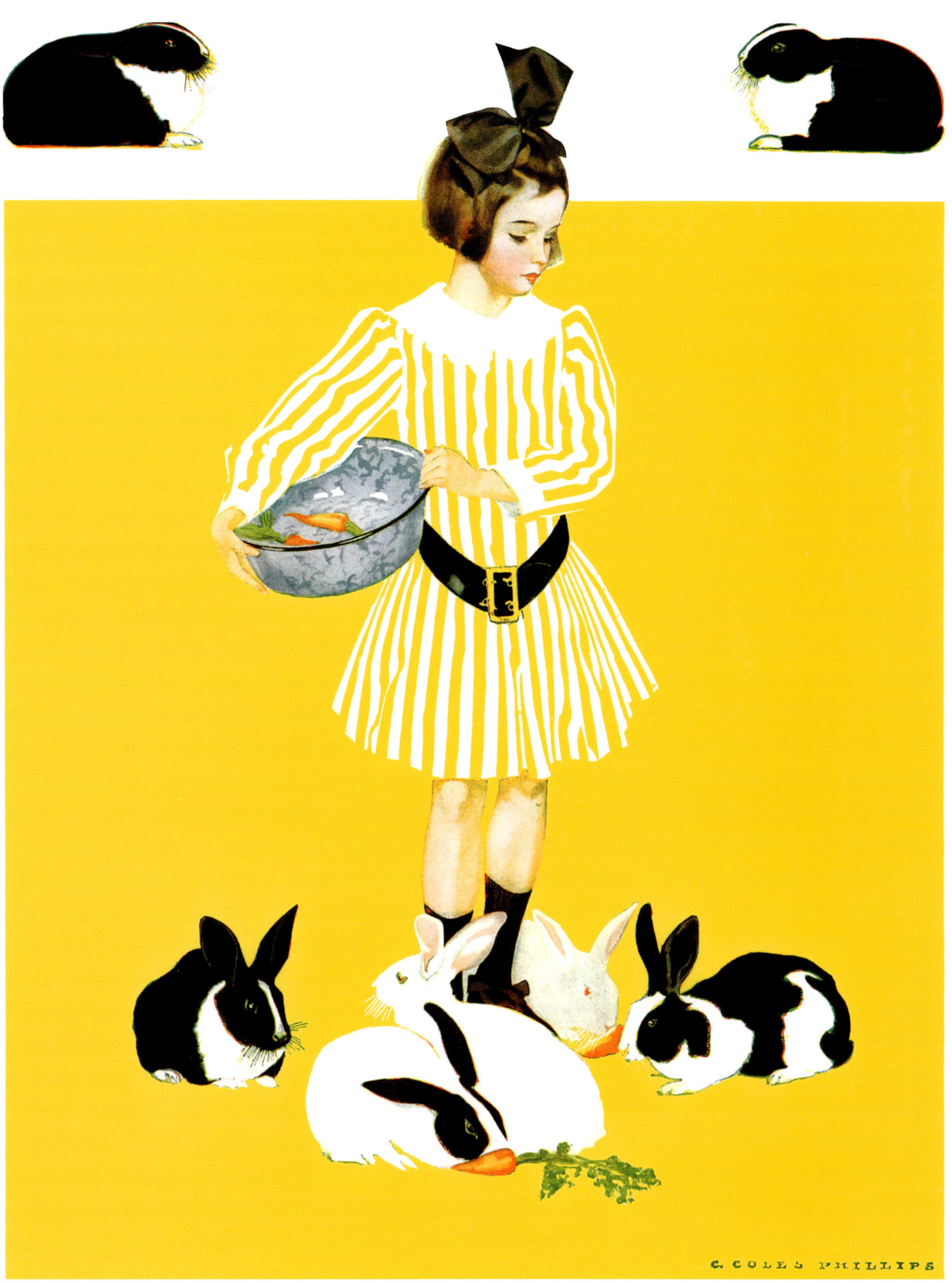

7. *A Friend of the Family*
Cover art from *Life* Magazine, April 6, 1911

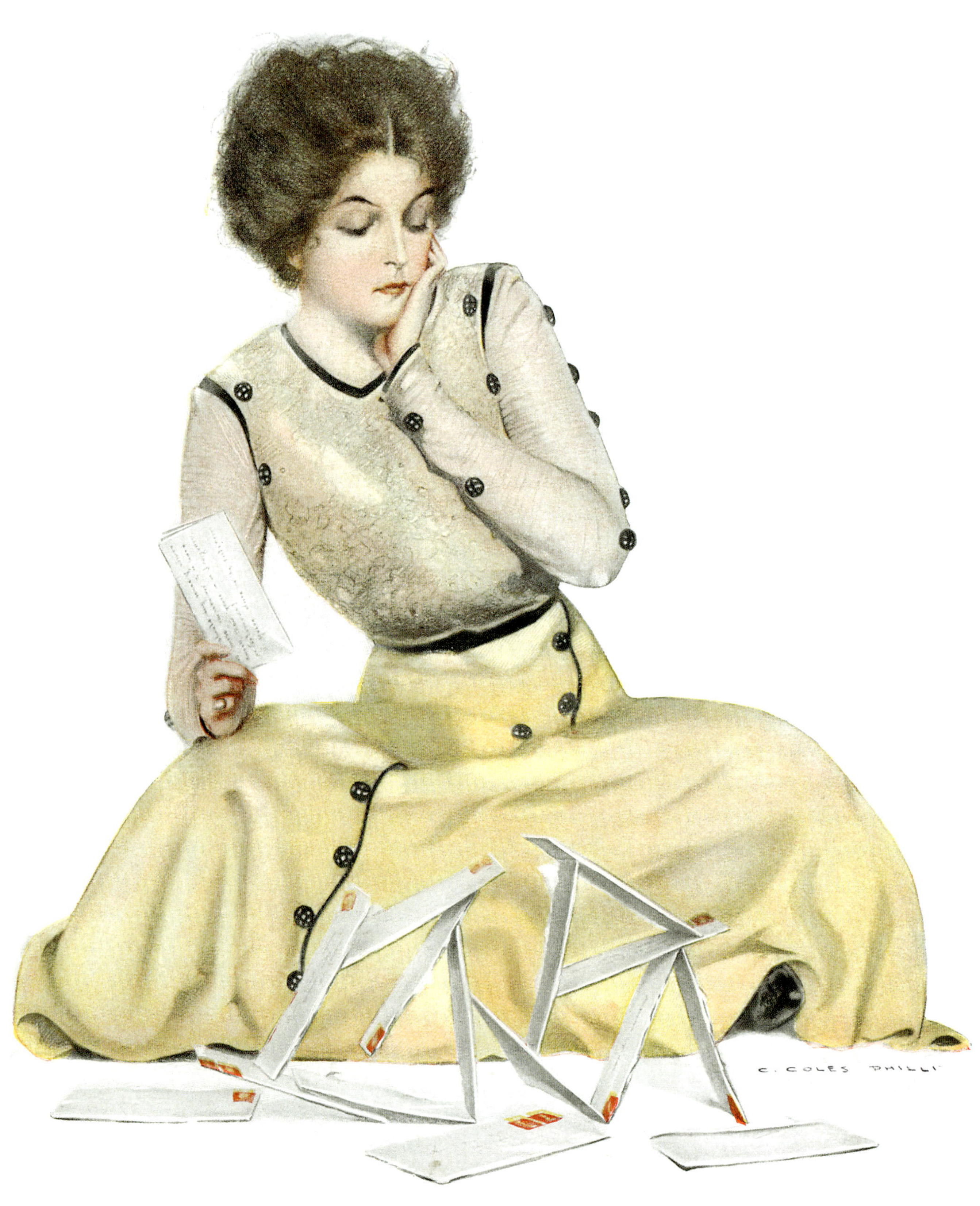

8. *The House That Jack Built*
Cover art from *Life* Magazine, March 31, 1910

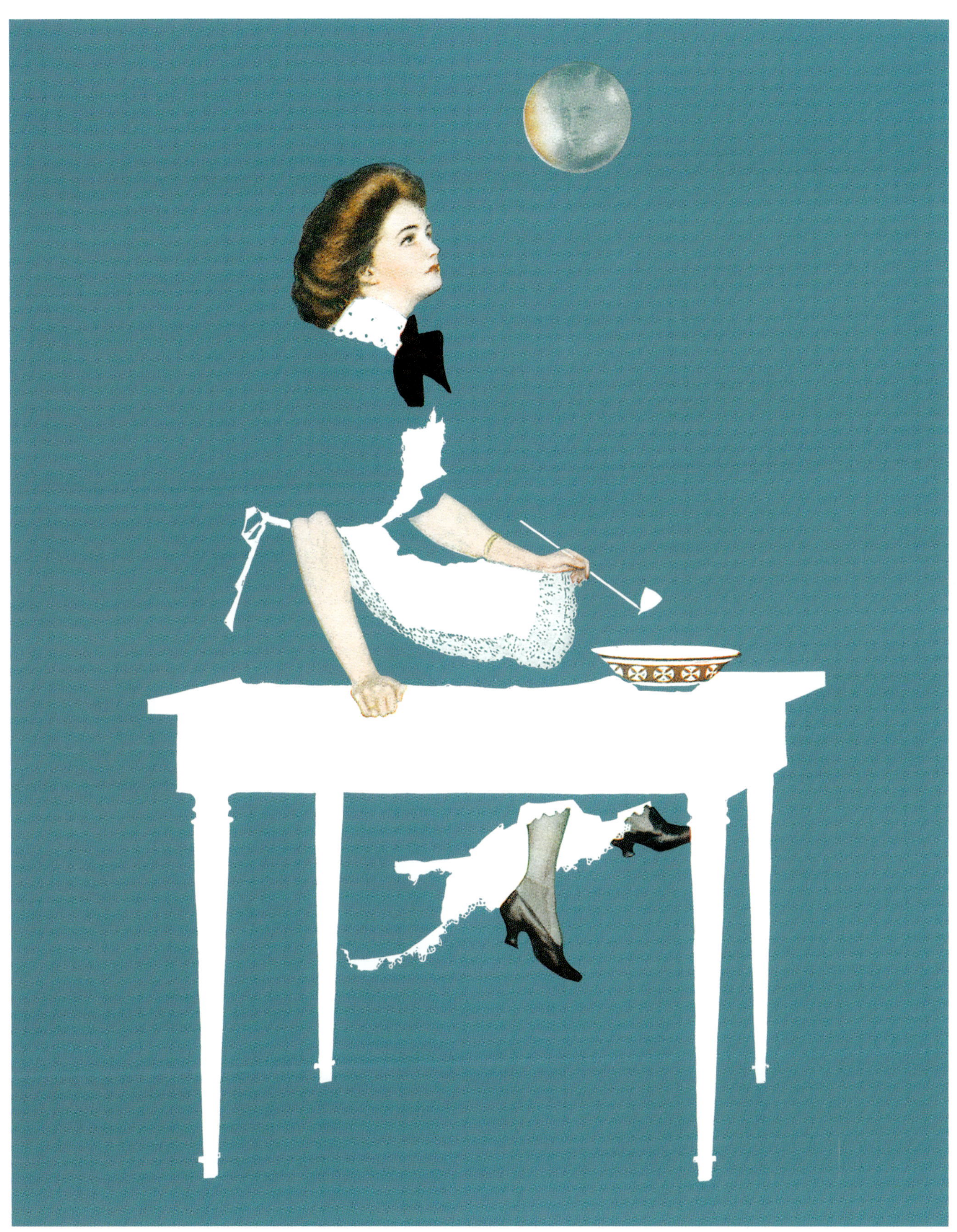

9. *Illusion*
Life Magazine, 1911

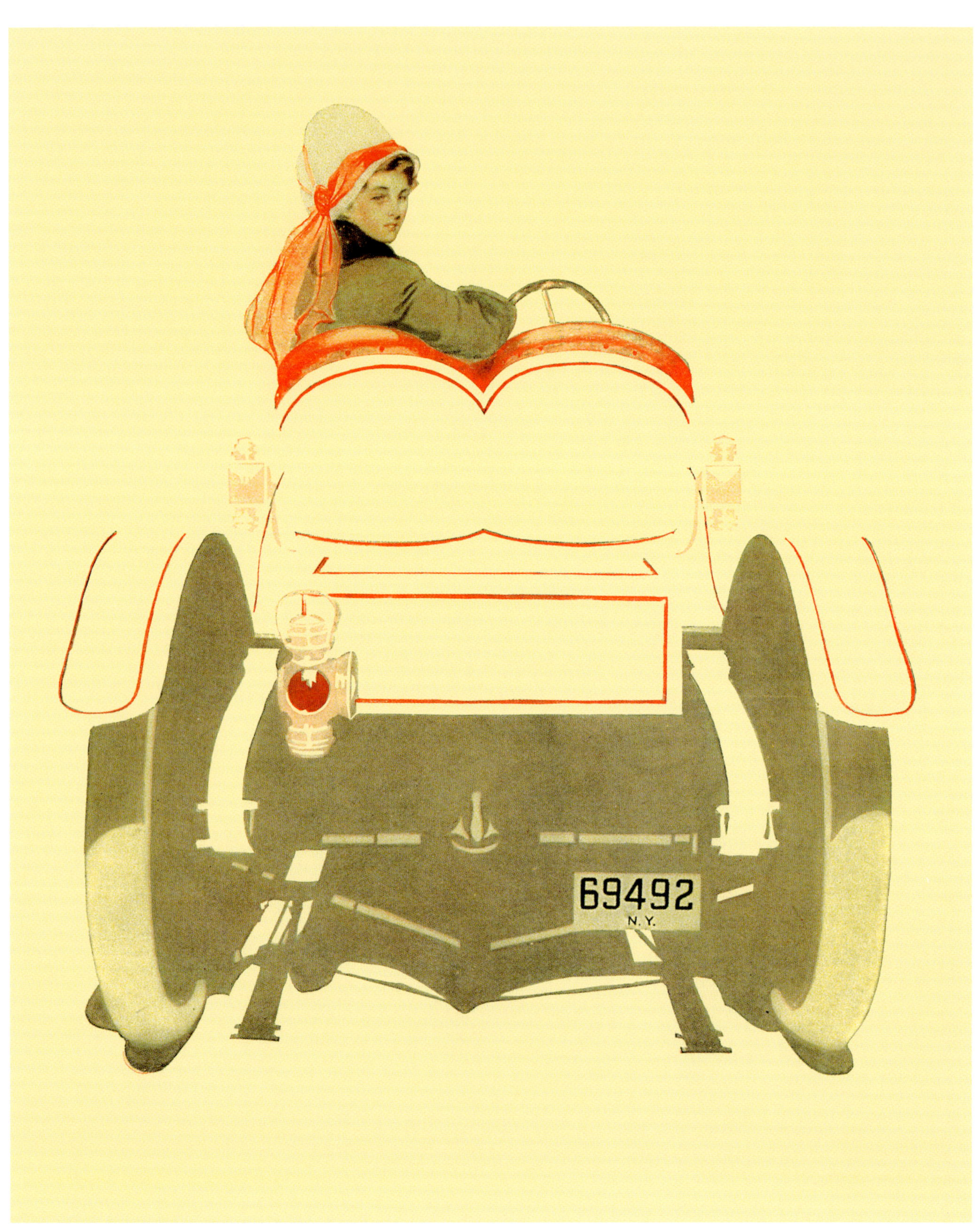

10. *One Girl Power*
Cover art from *Life* Magazine, January 6, 1910

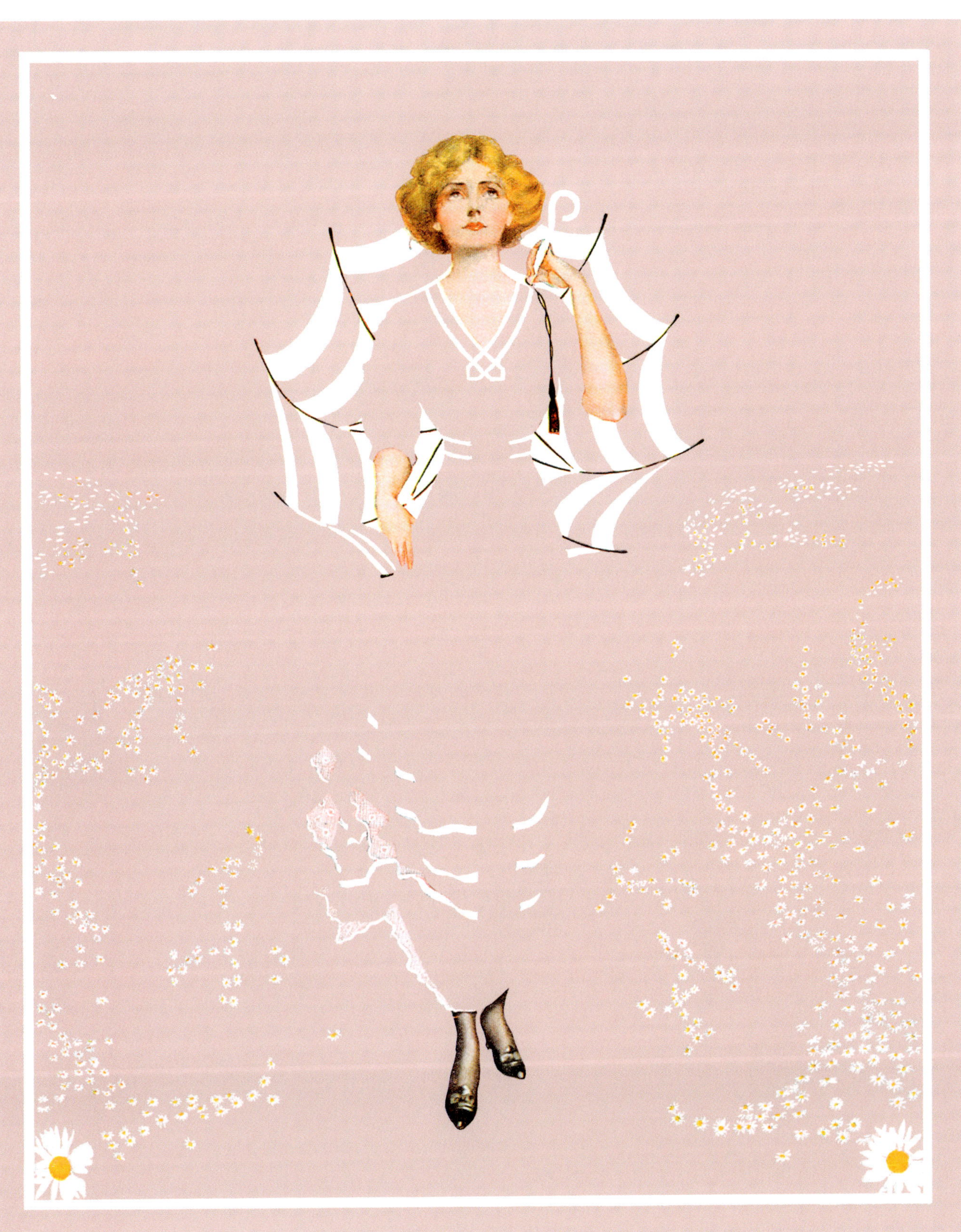

11. *Even the Daisies of the Field*
Cover art from *Life* Magazine, March 3, 1910

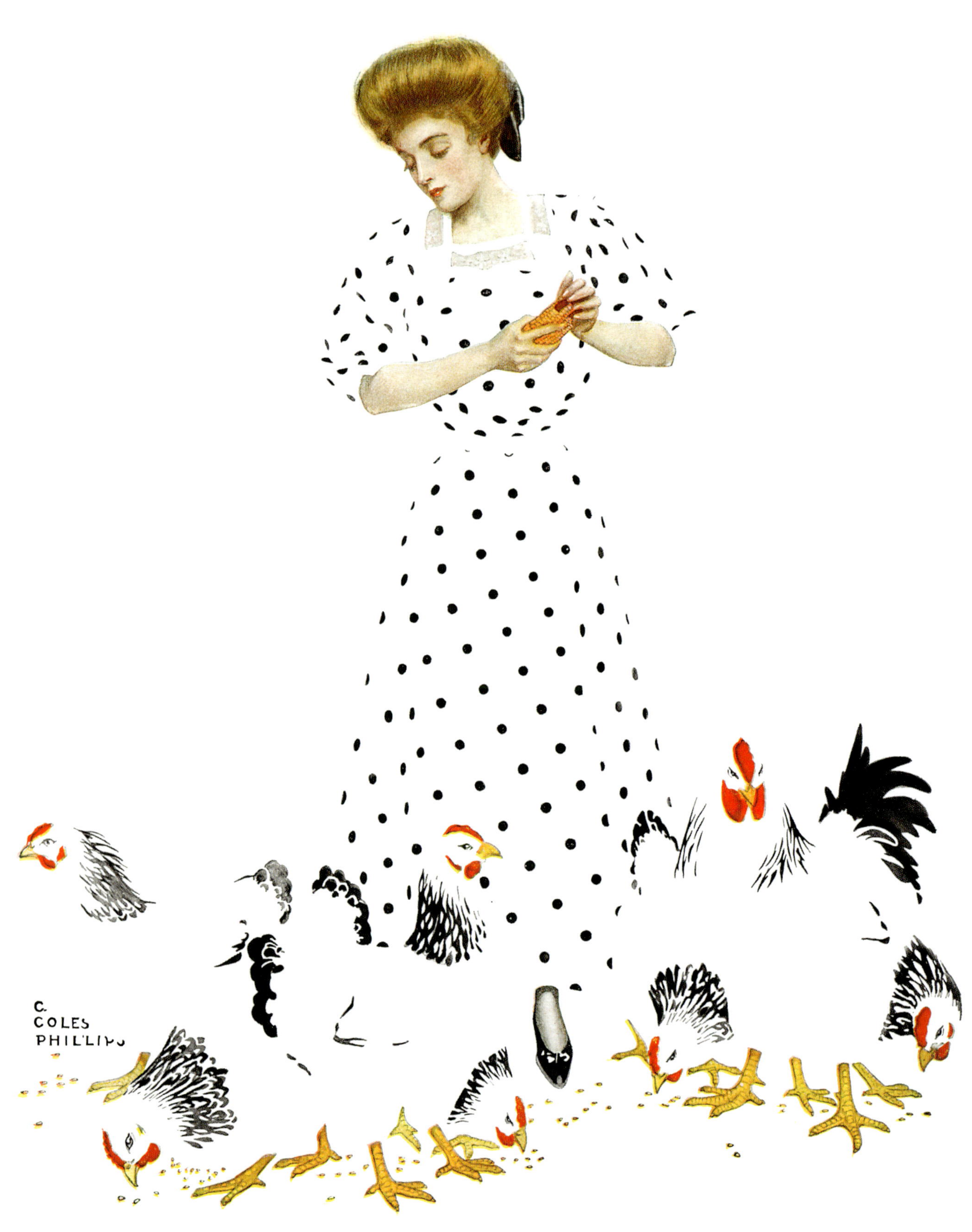

12. *Corn Exchange*
Cover art from *Life* Magazine, May 28, 1910

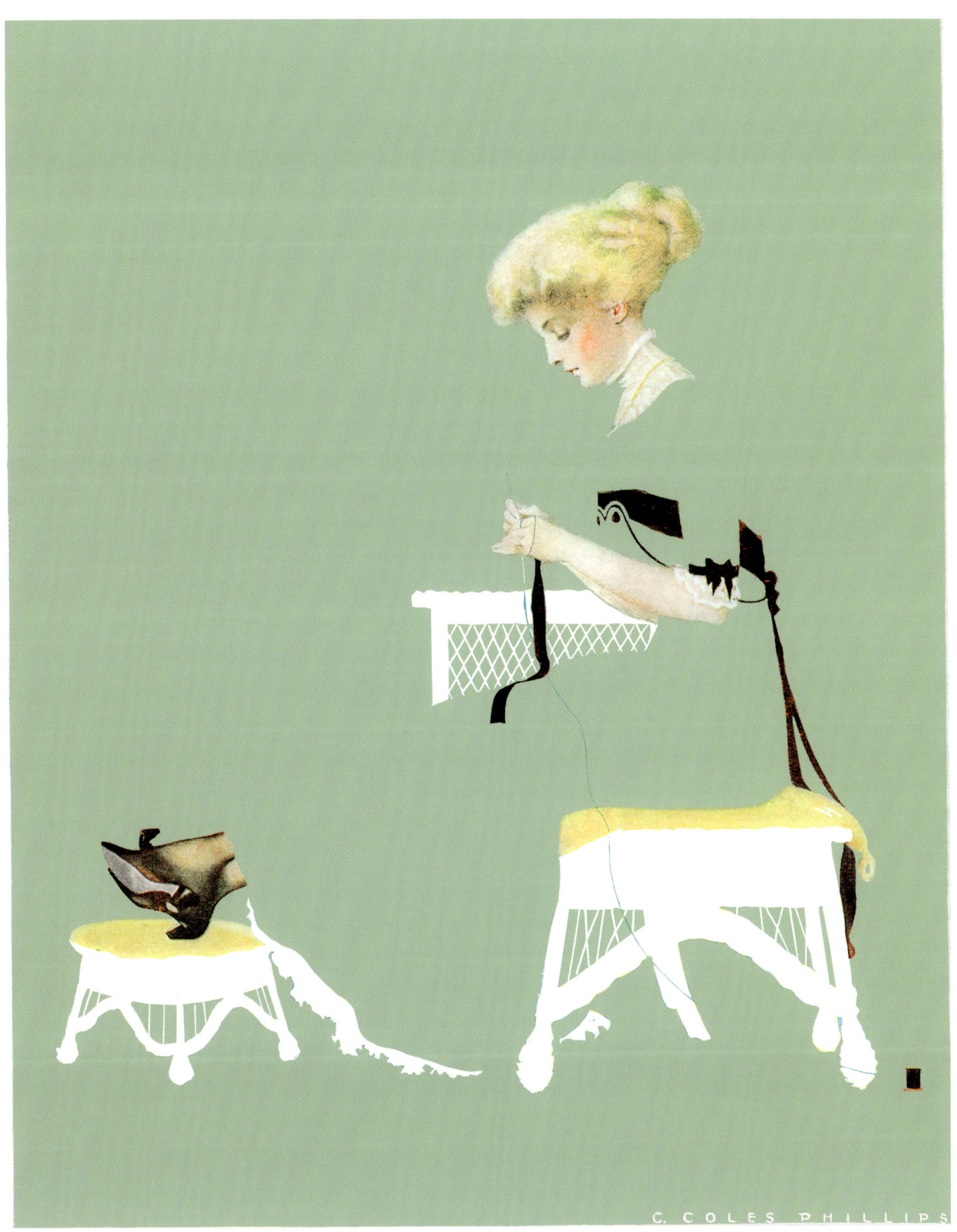

13. *Home Ties*
Cover art from *Life* Magazine, October 14, 1909

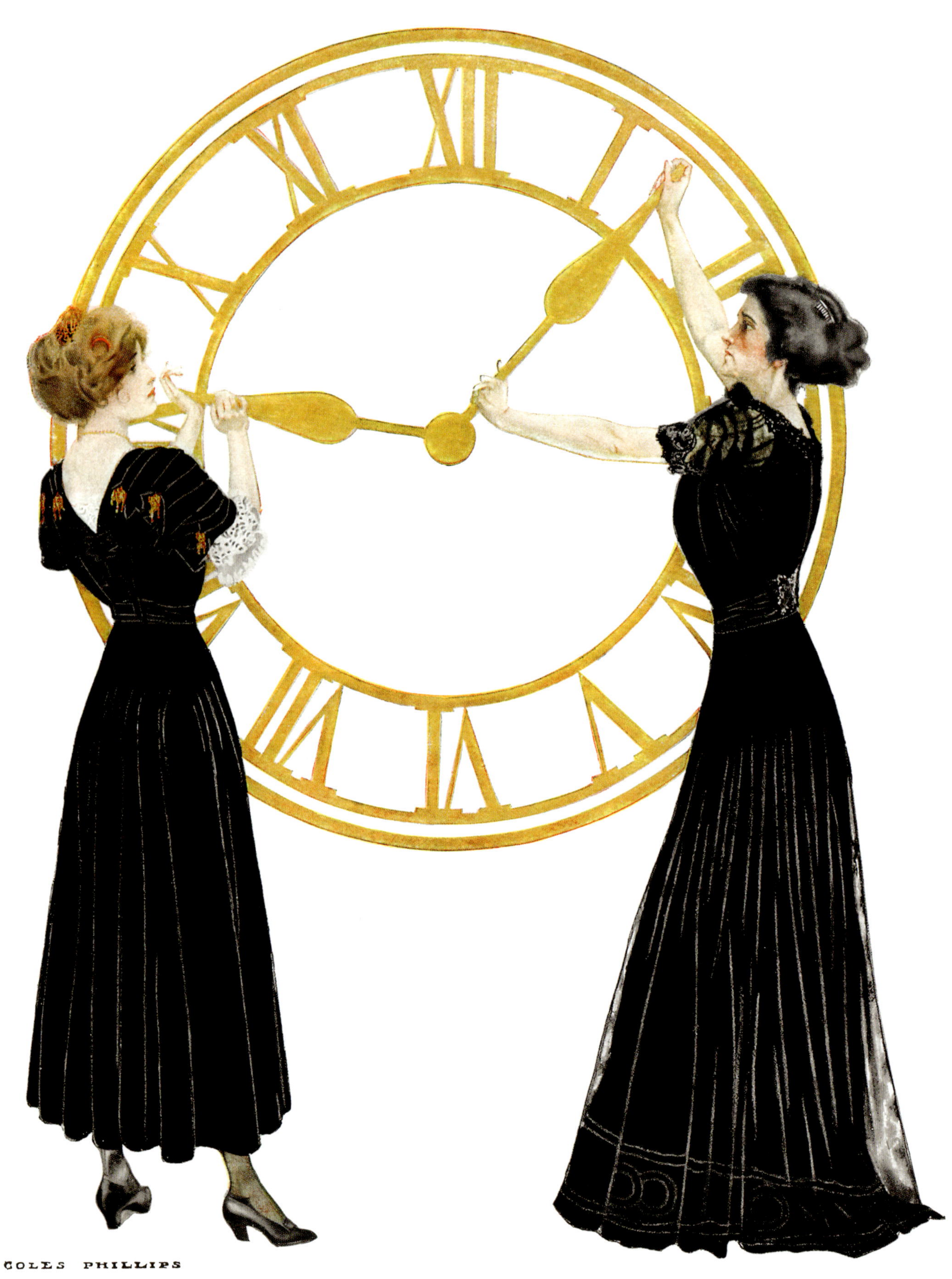

14. *Forward and Back*
Cover art from *Life* Magazine, March 16, 1911

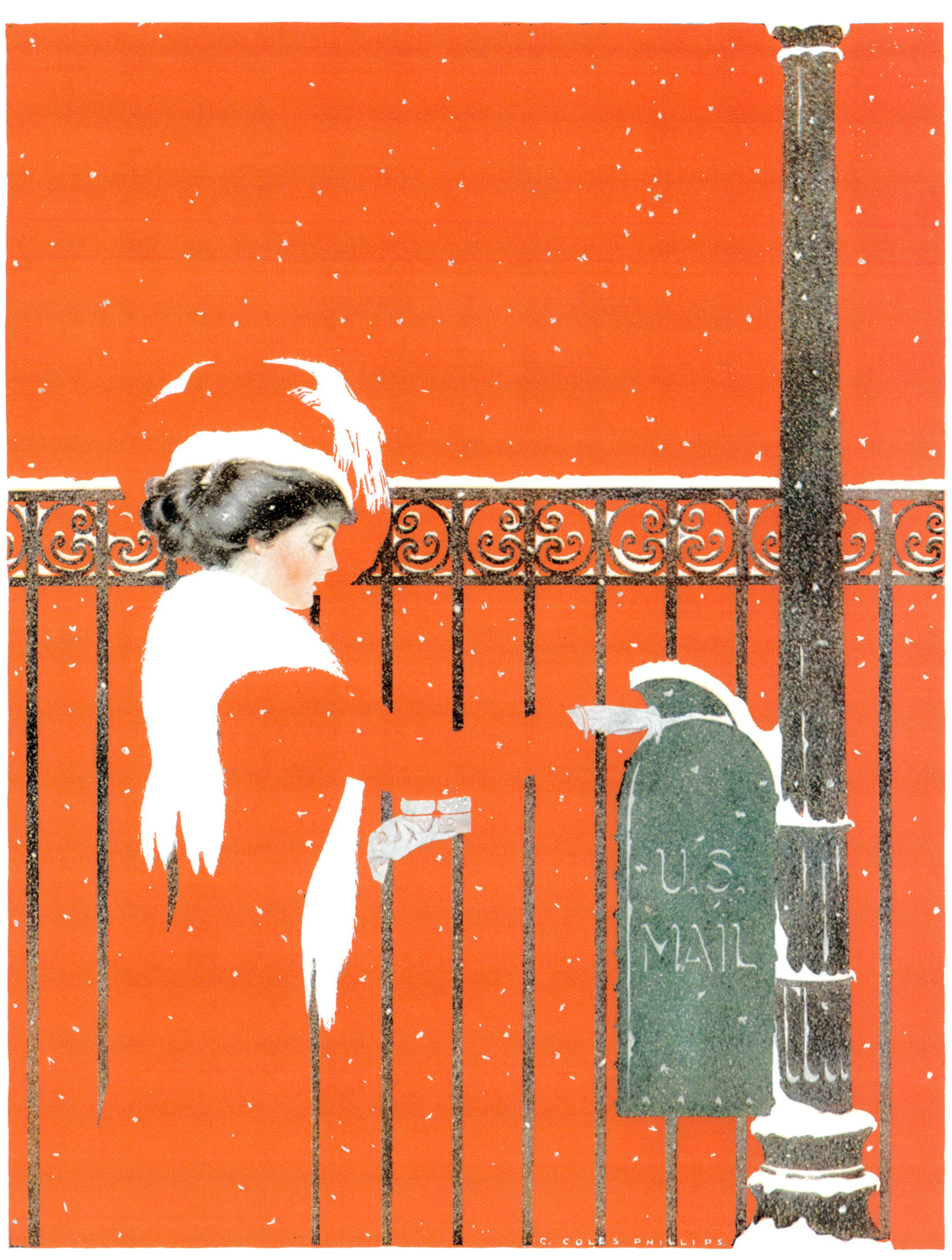

15. *Between You and Me and the Post*
Cover art from *Life* Magazine, December 2, 1909

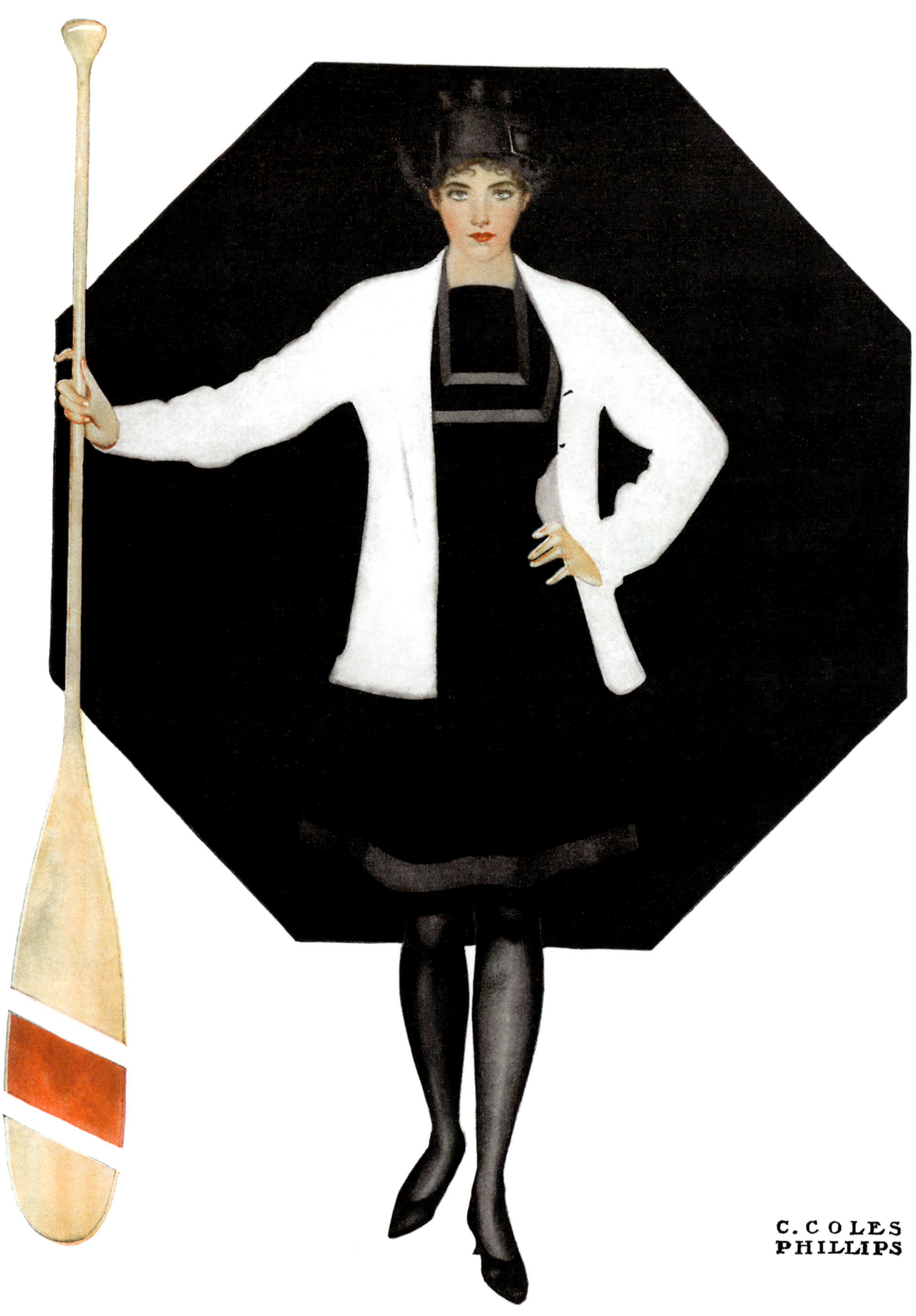

16. *A Call to Arms* or *A Safe Guide?*
Cover art from *Life* Magazine, July 27, 1911

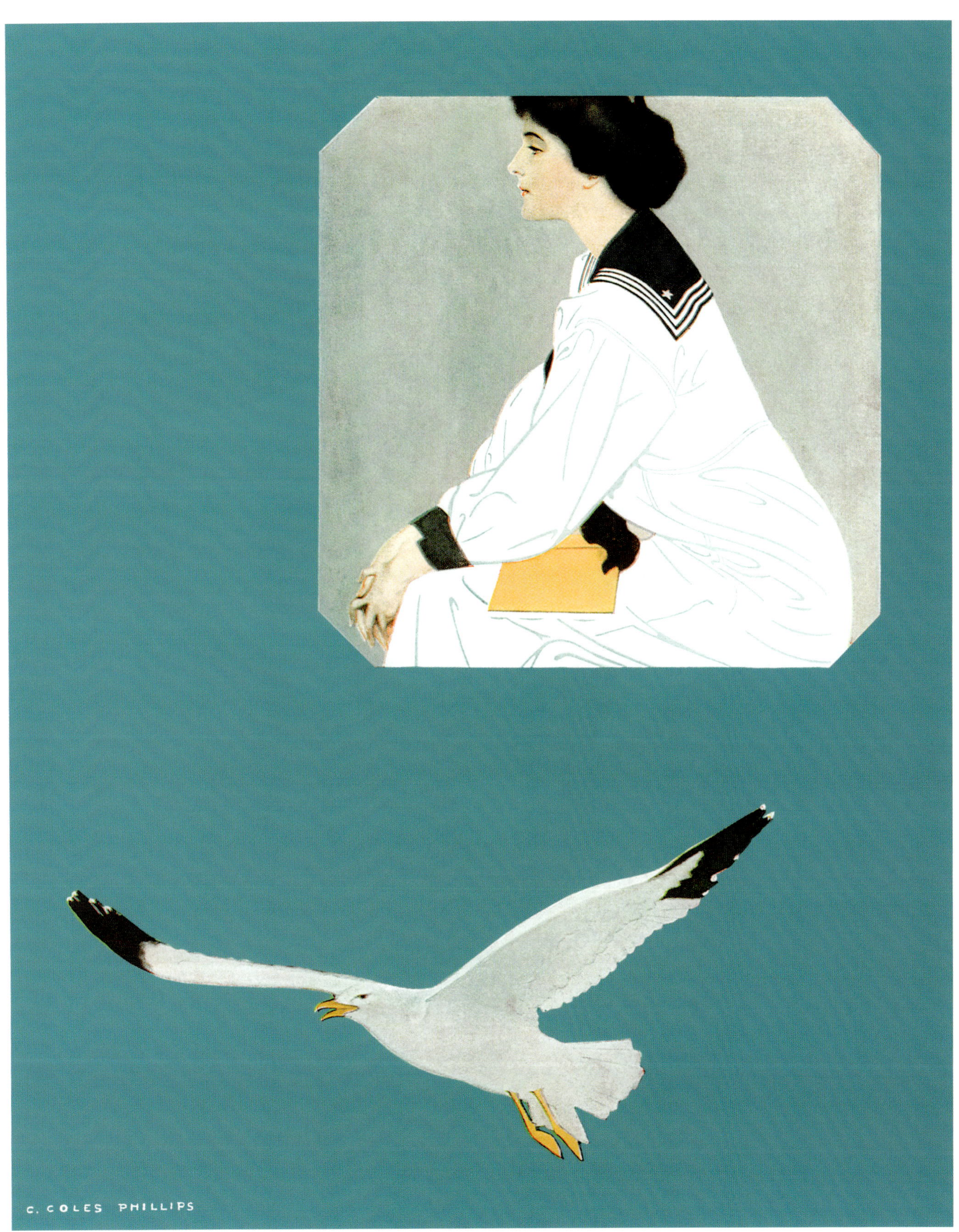

17. *The Lass that Loved a Sailor*
Cover art from *Life* Magazine, August 18, 1910

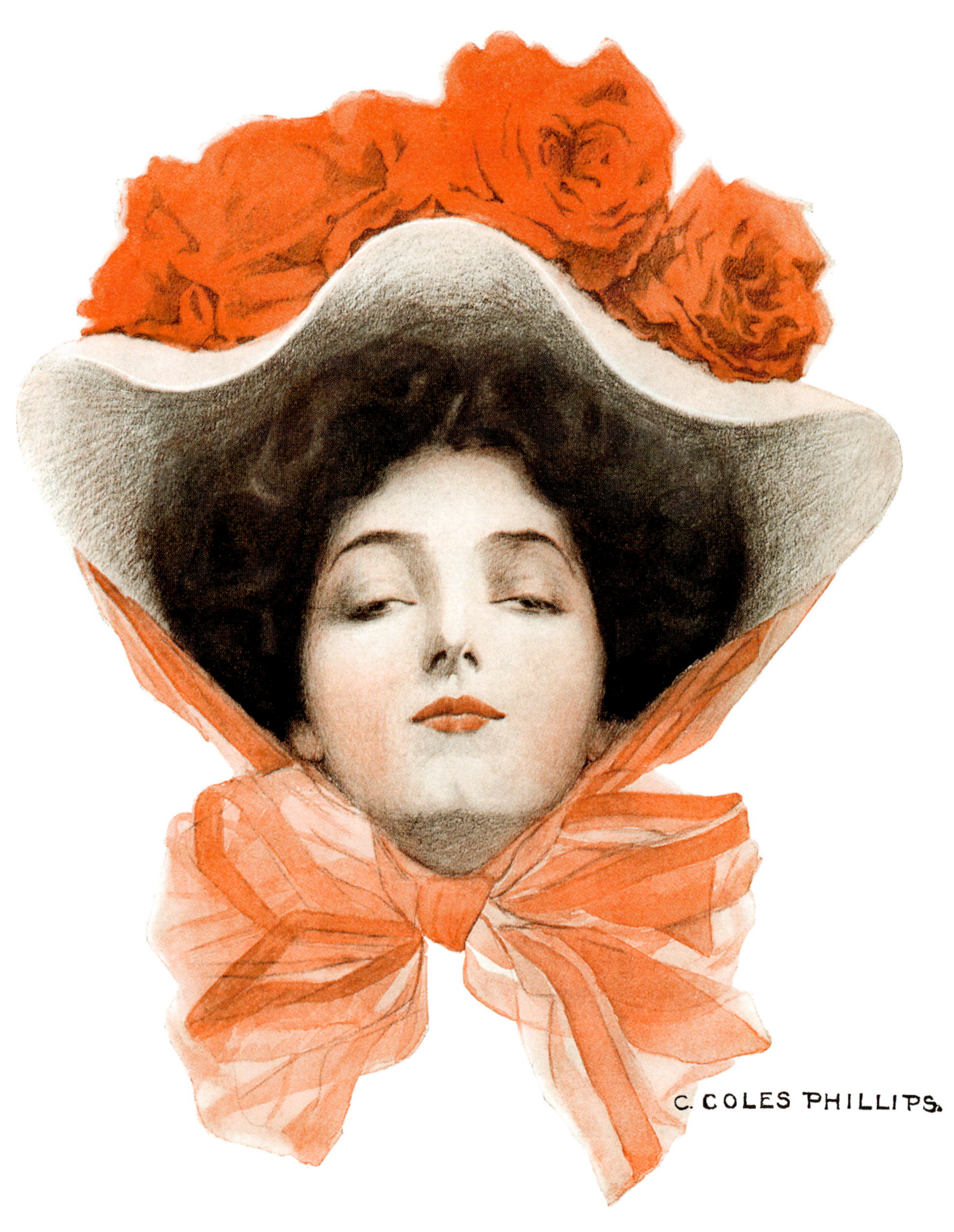

18. *R. S. V. P.*
Cover art from *Life* Magazine, March 12, 1908

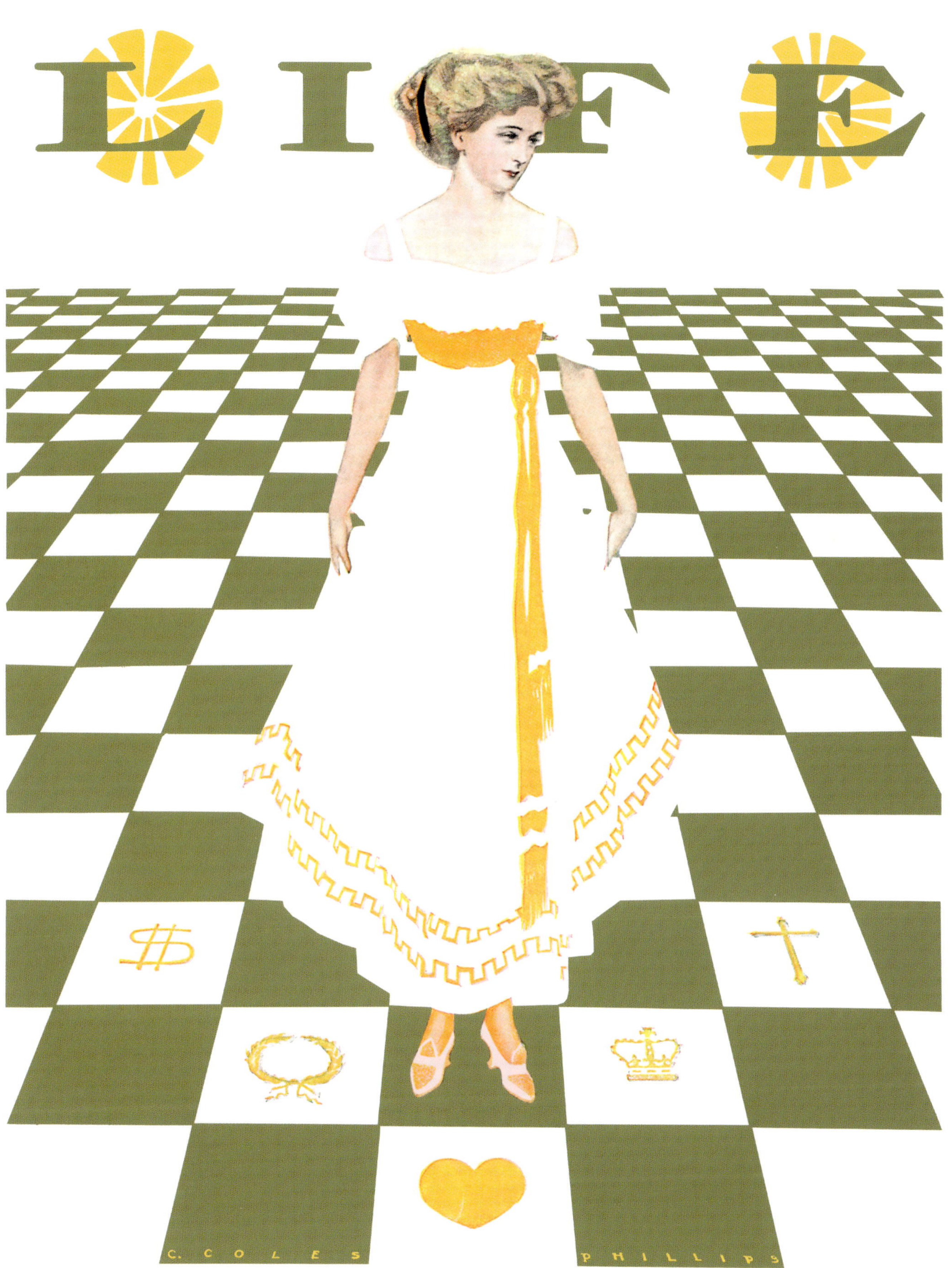

19. *Her Move*
Cover art from *Life* Magazine, June 10, 1909

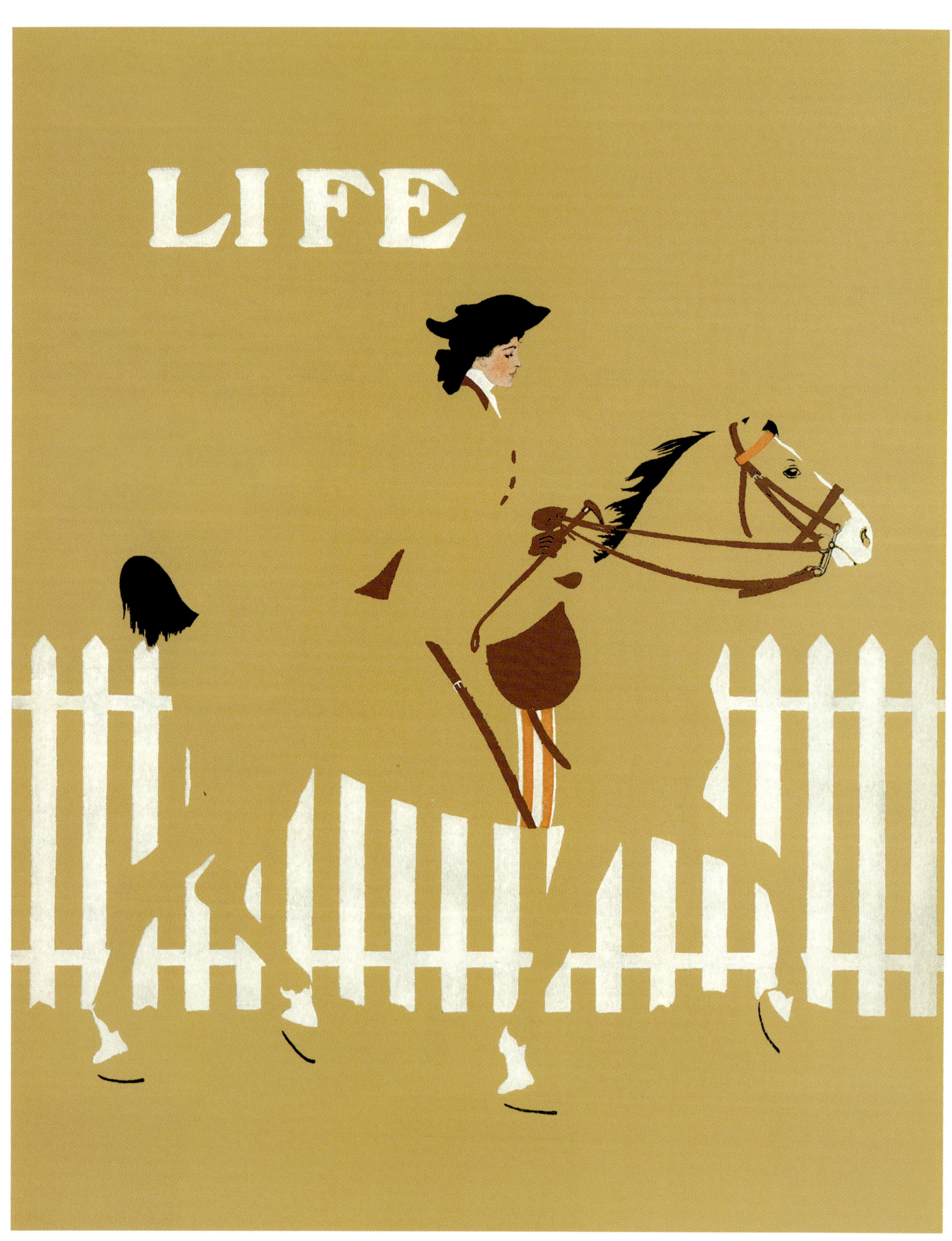

20. *Thoroughbreds*
Cover art from *Life* Magazine, November 12, 1908

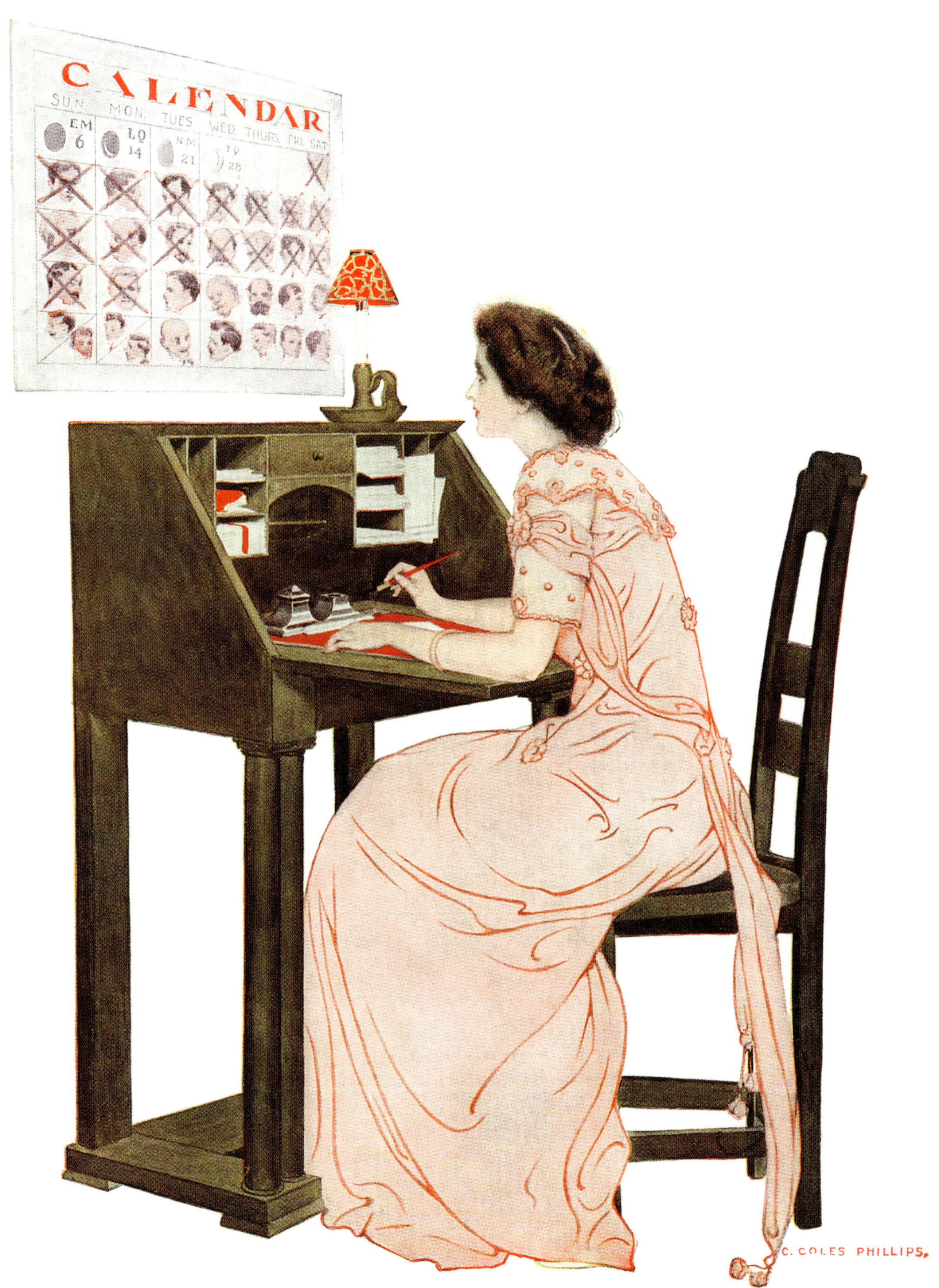

21. *Dates*
Cover art from *Life* Magazine, September 23, 1909

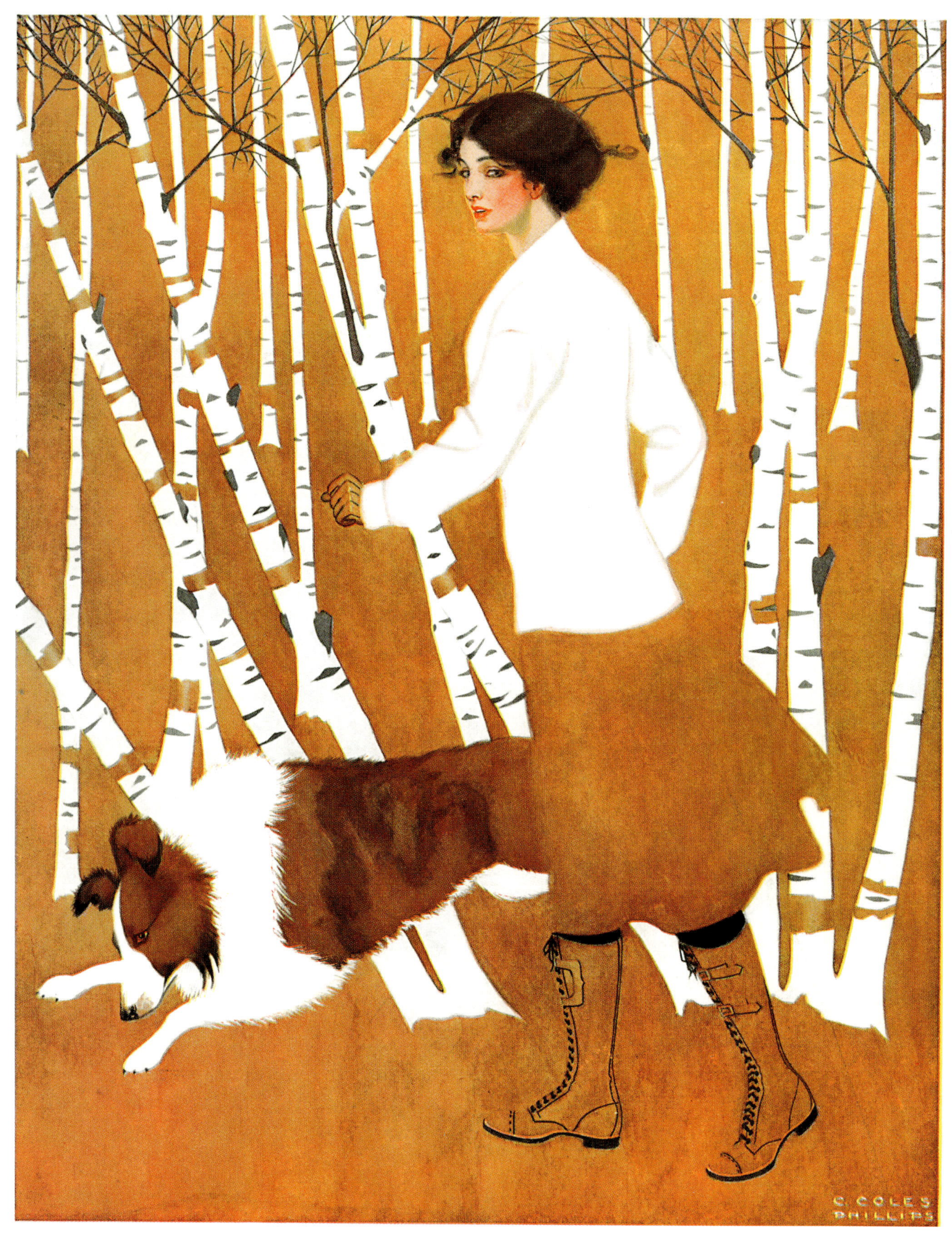

22. *Birches*
Cover art from *Life* Magazine, October 28, 1911

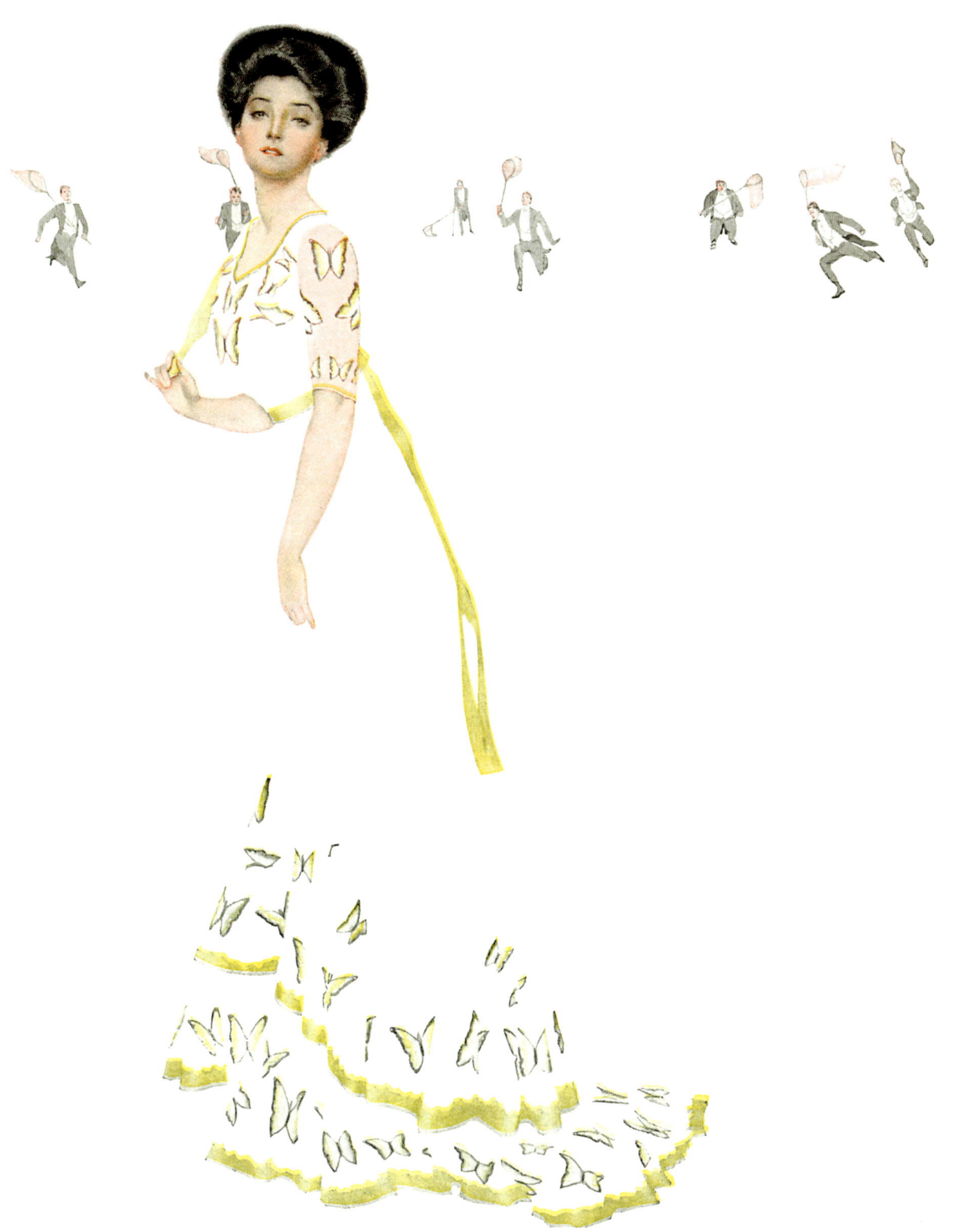

23. *The Butterfly Chase*
Cover art from *Life* Magazine, March 10, 1910

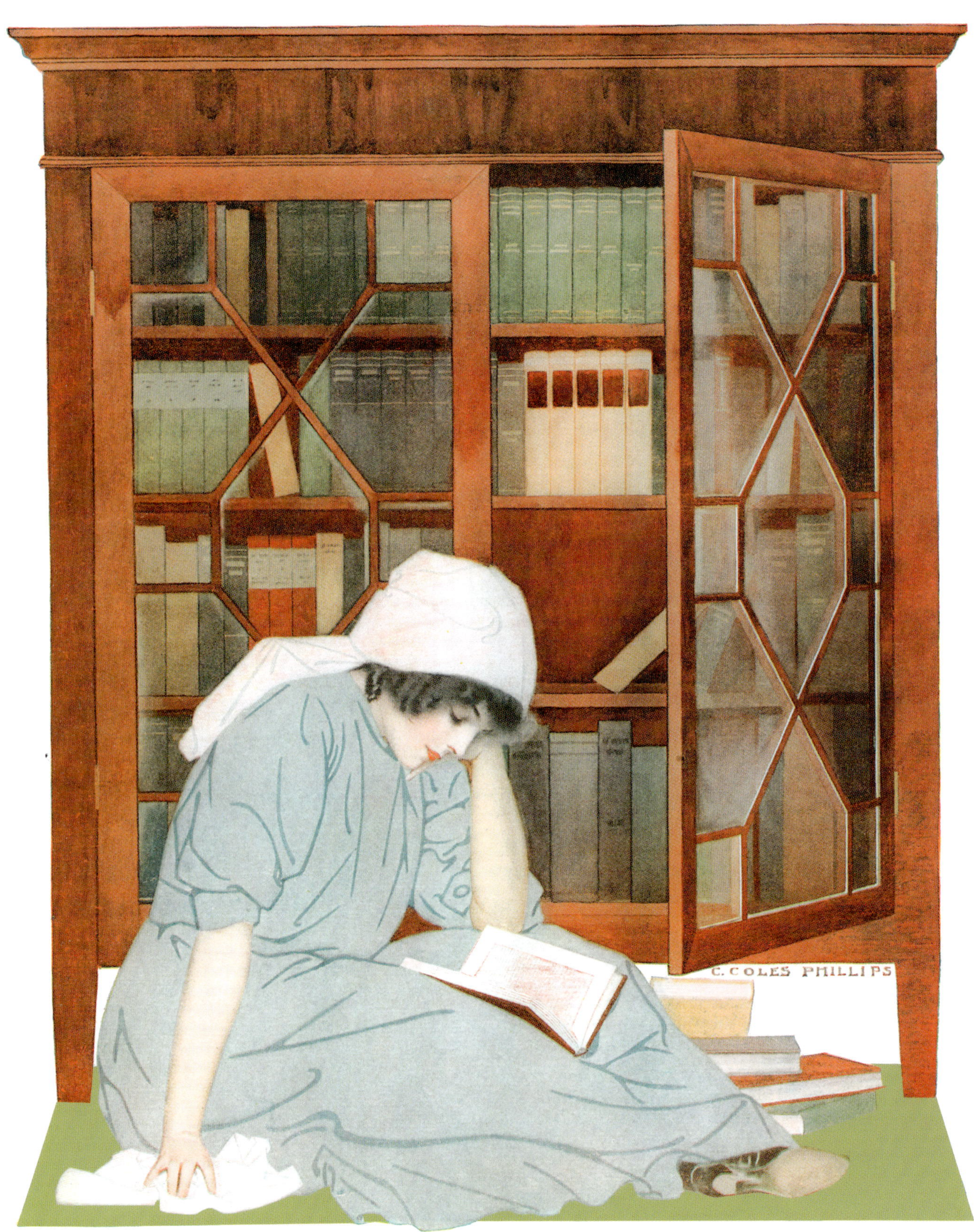

24. *The Lure of Books*
Cover art from *Life* Magazine, June 8, 1911

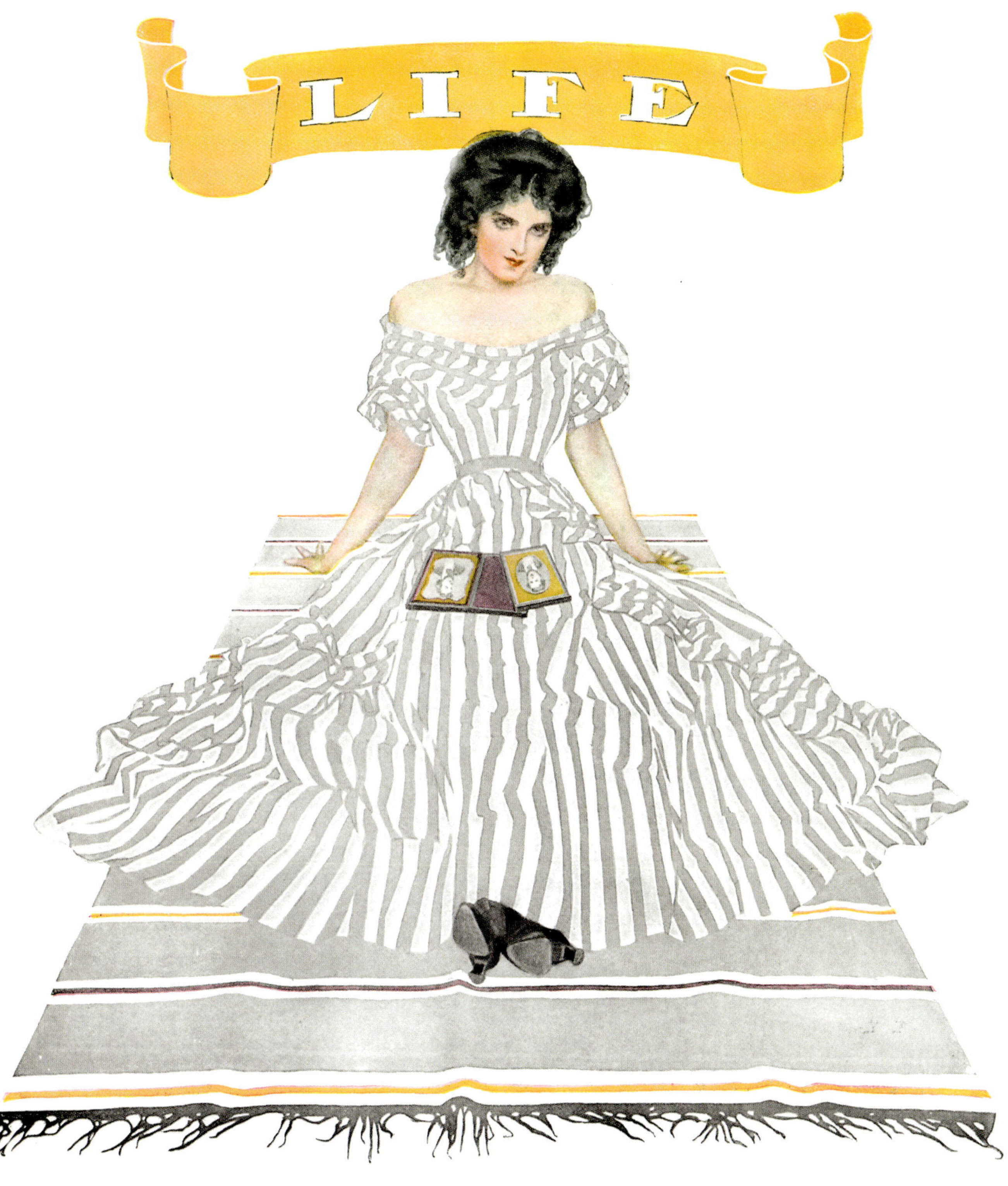

25. *Which?*
Cover art from *Life* Magazine, July 15, 1909

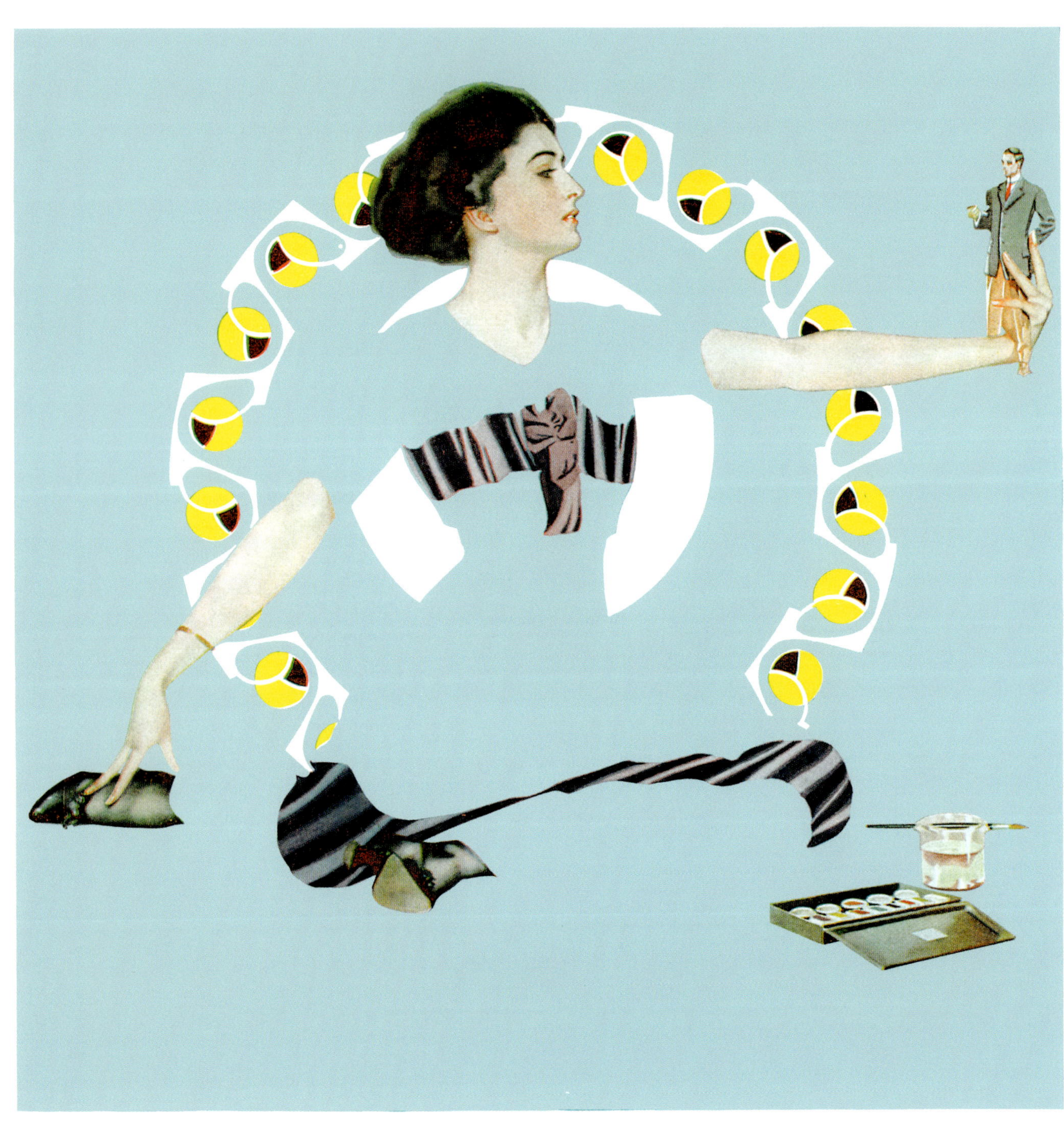

26. *Idol Industry* or *A Troublesome Toy*
Cover art from *Life* Magazine, September 28, 1911

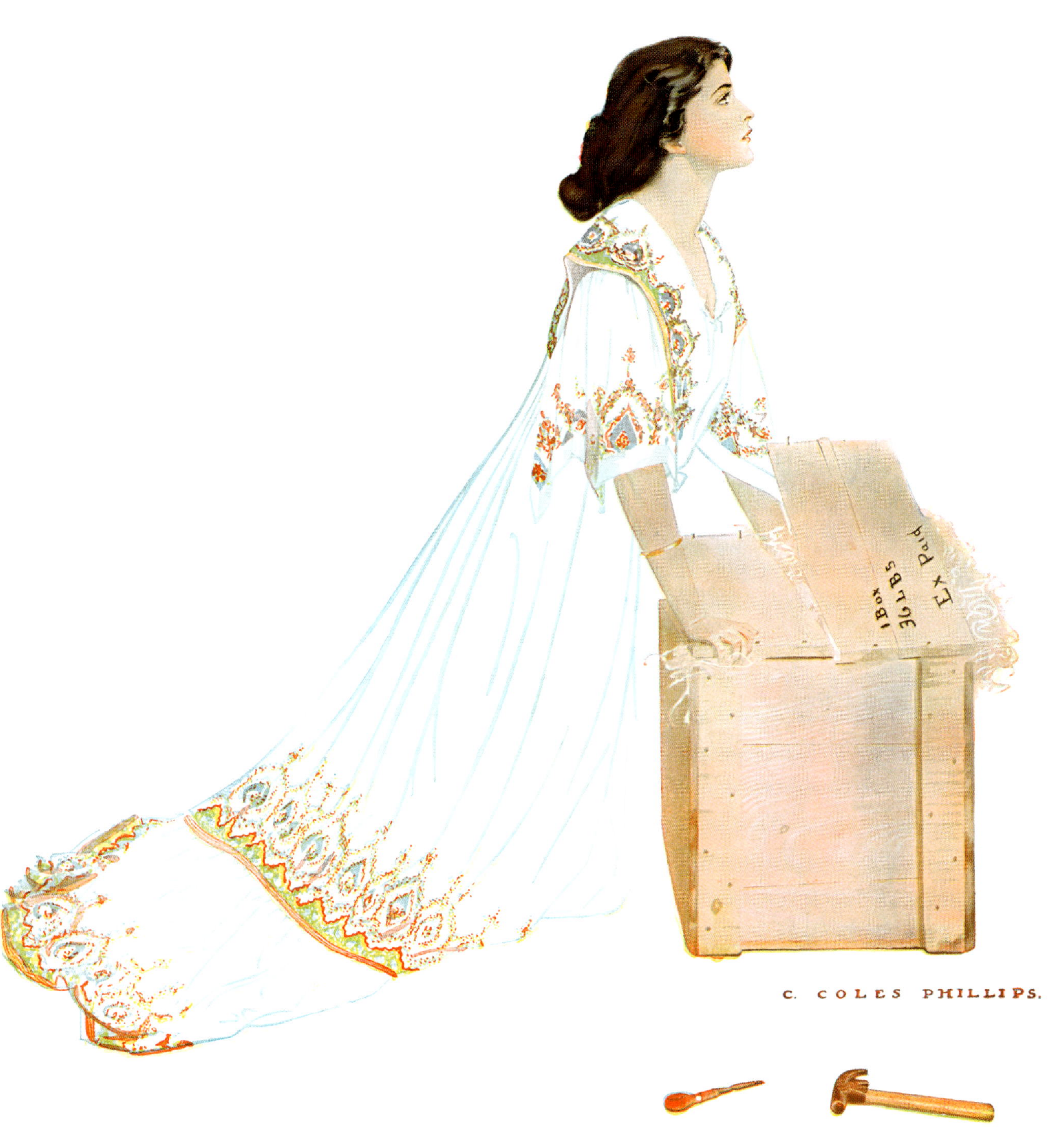

27. *Christmas Box Party* or *The Absent One*
Cover art from *Life* Magazine, December 1, 1910

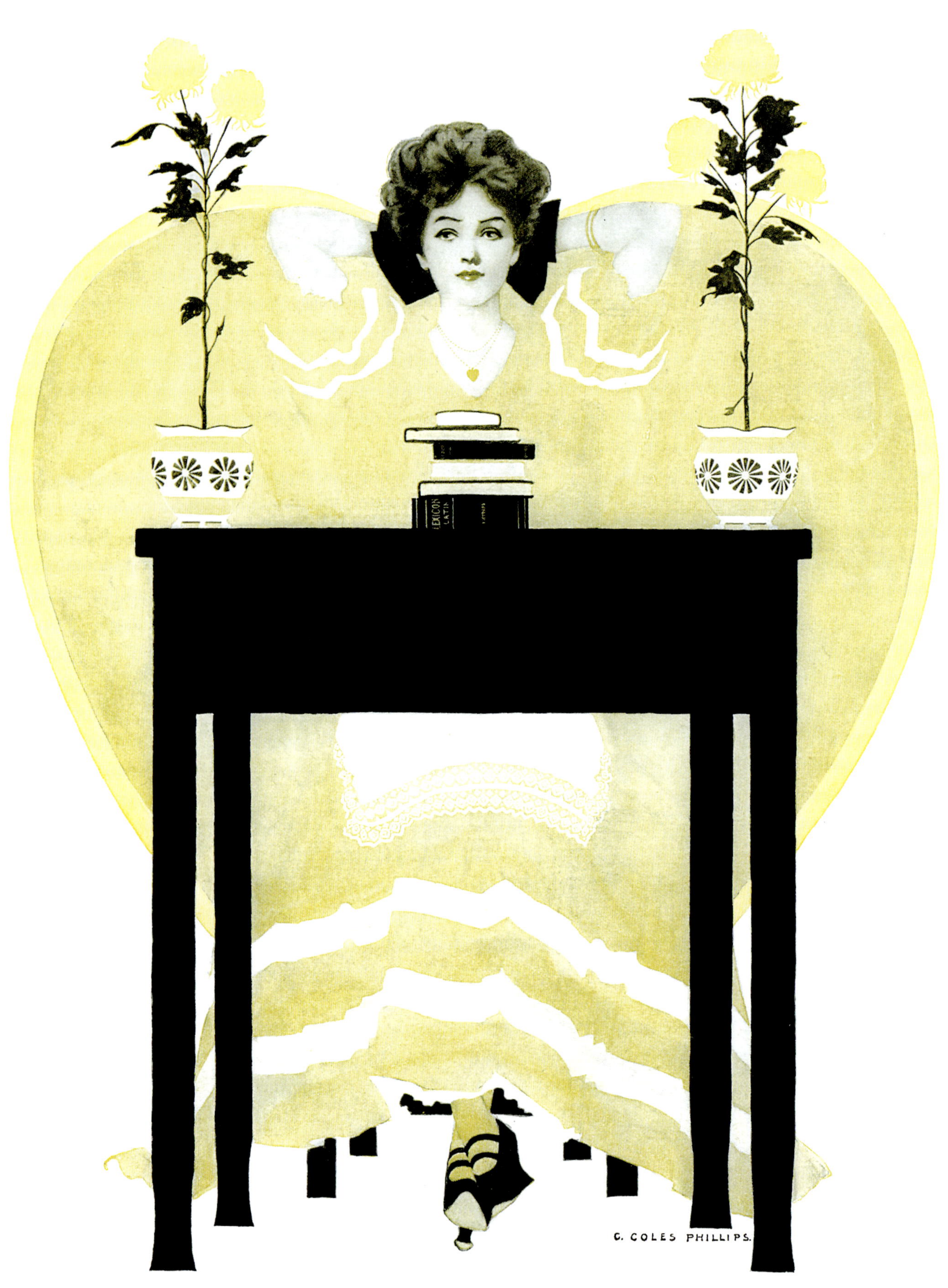

28. *On the Threshold*
Cover art from *Life* Magazine, May 21, 1908

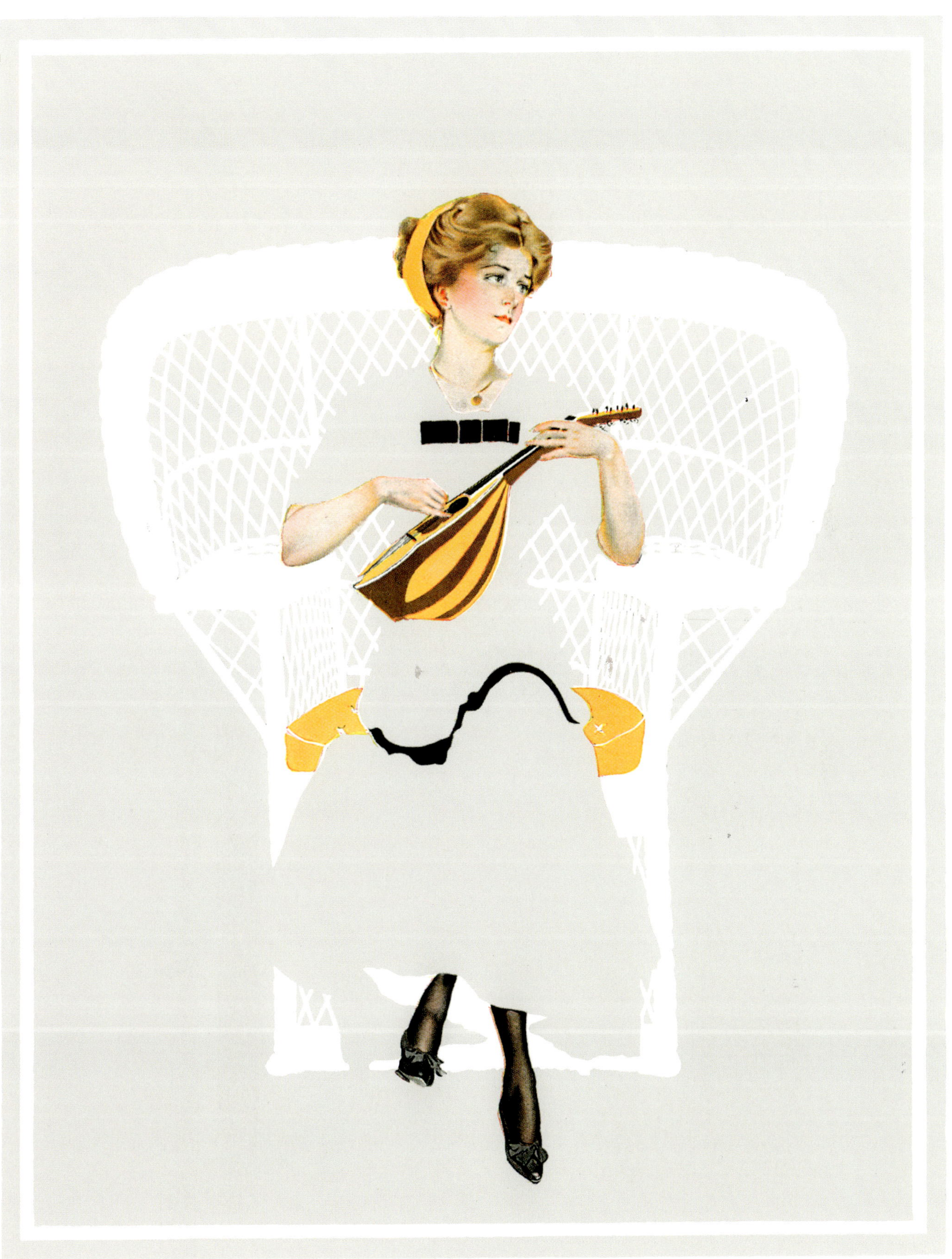

29. *Without Accompaniment*
Cover art from *Life* Magazine, June 15, 1911

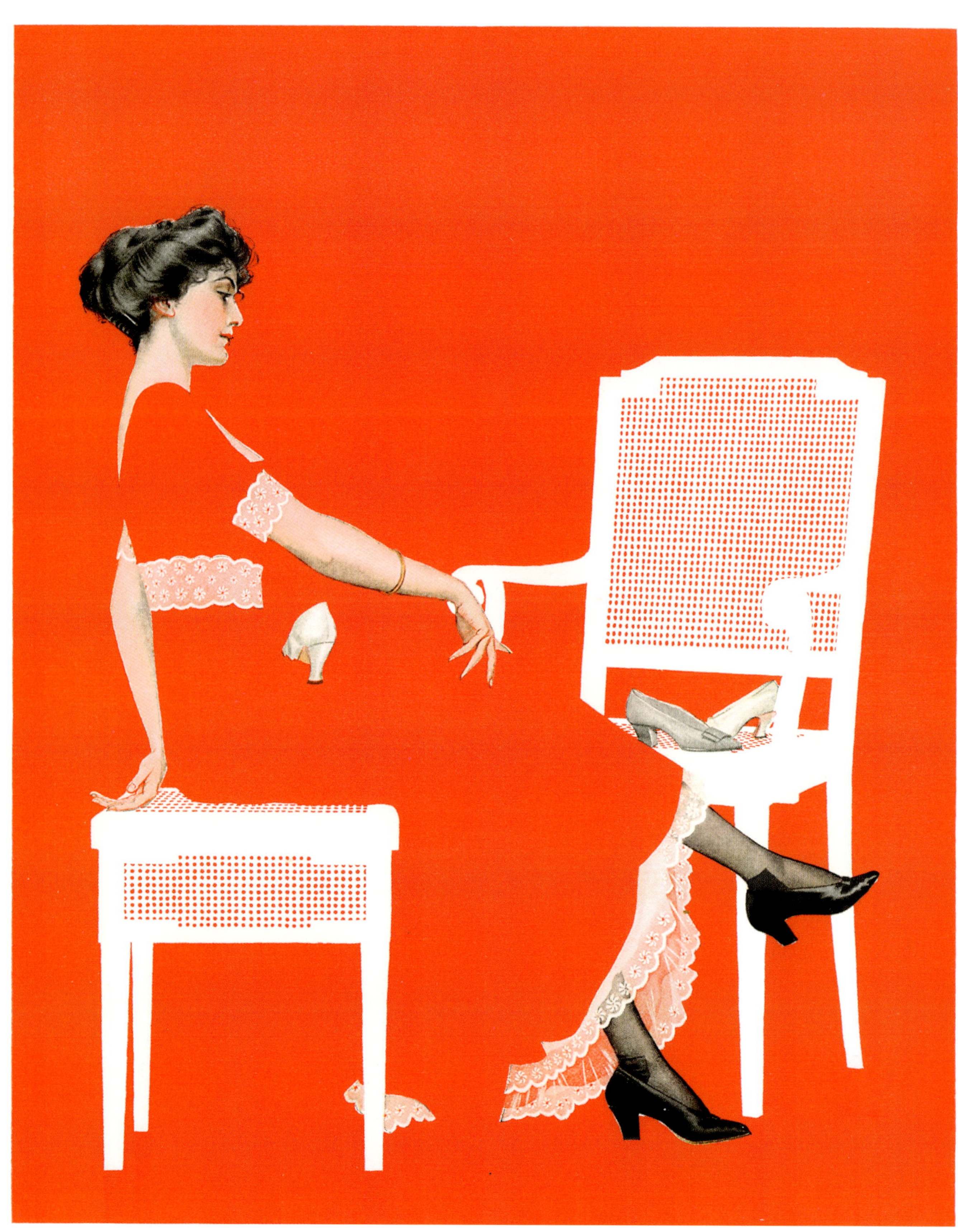

30. *The Survival of the Fittest*
Cover art from *Life* Magazine, August 31, 1911

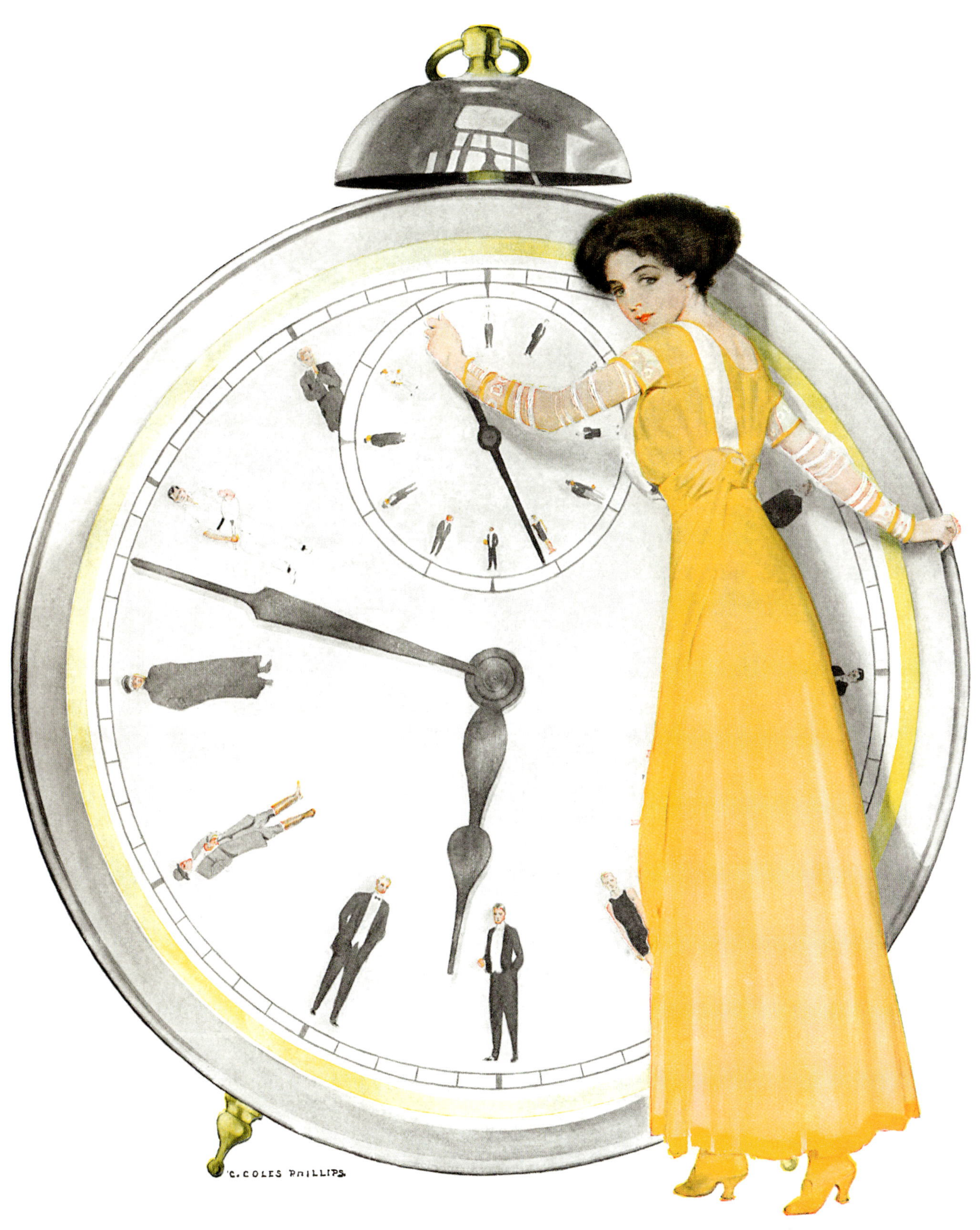

31. *The Time of Her life*
Cover art from *Life* Magazine, August 5, 1909

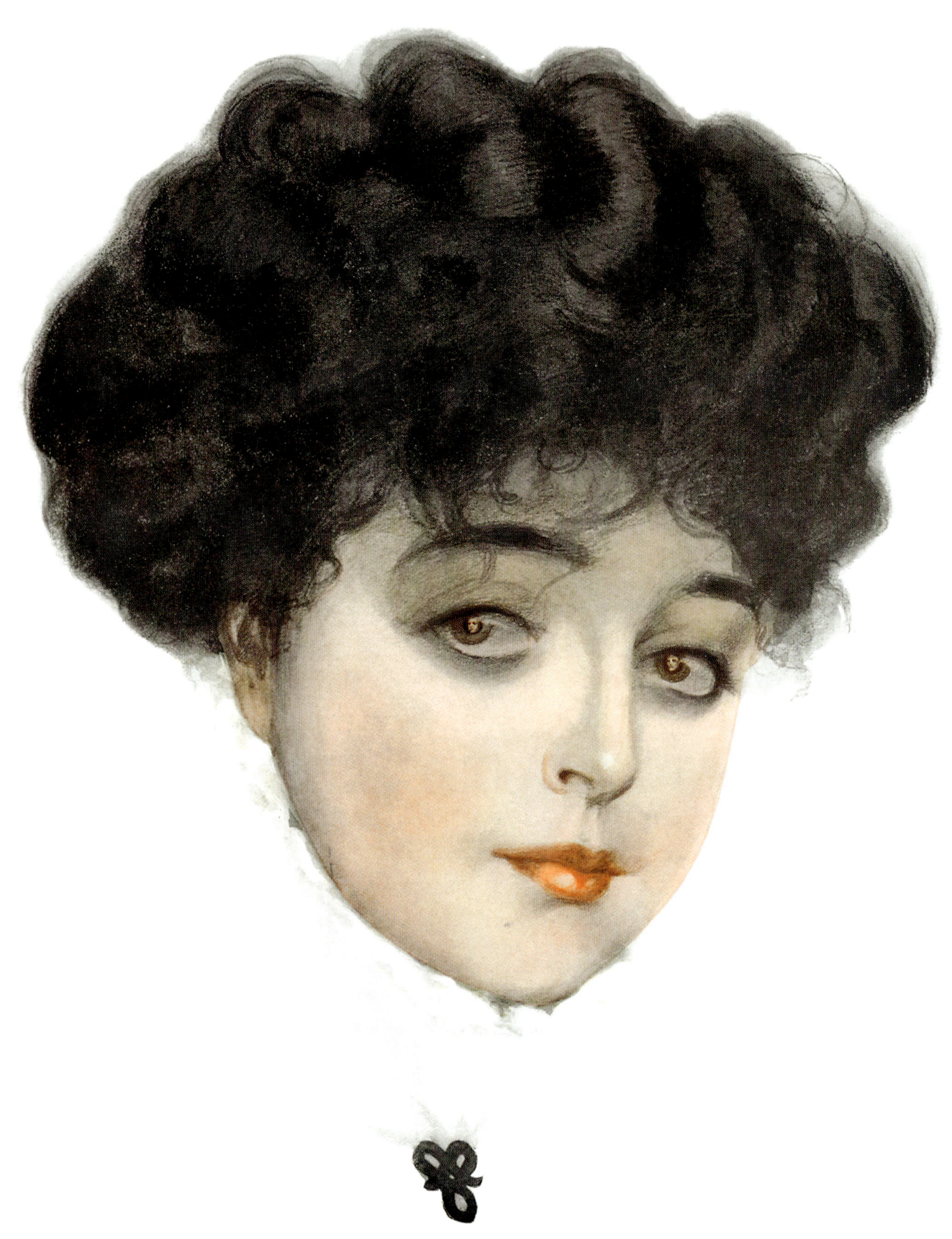

32. *Reflections of a Bachelor*
Cover art from *Life* Magazine, April 28, 1910

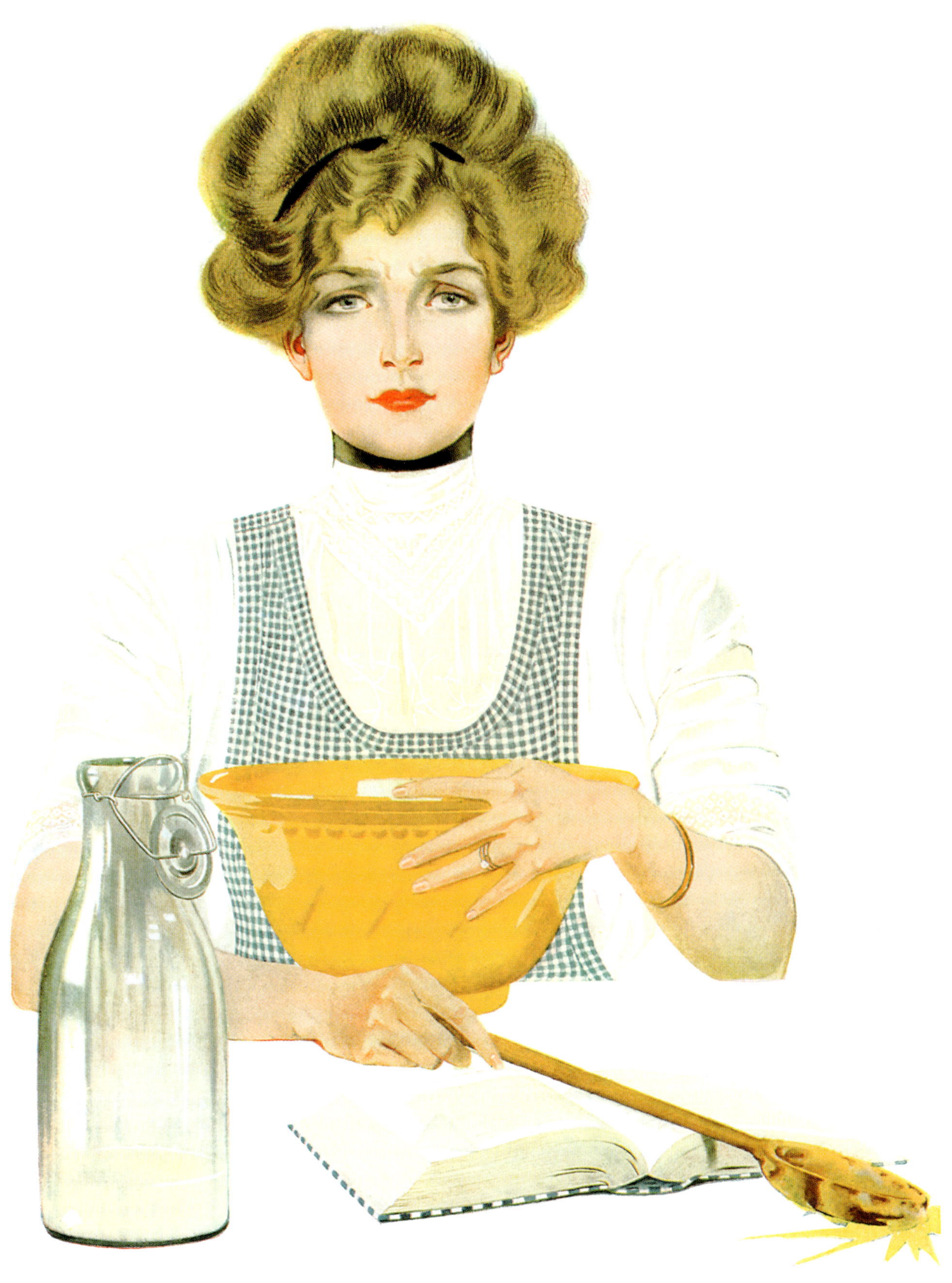

33. *The Light Housekeeper*
Cover art from *Life* Magazine, October 12, 1911

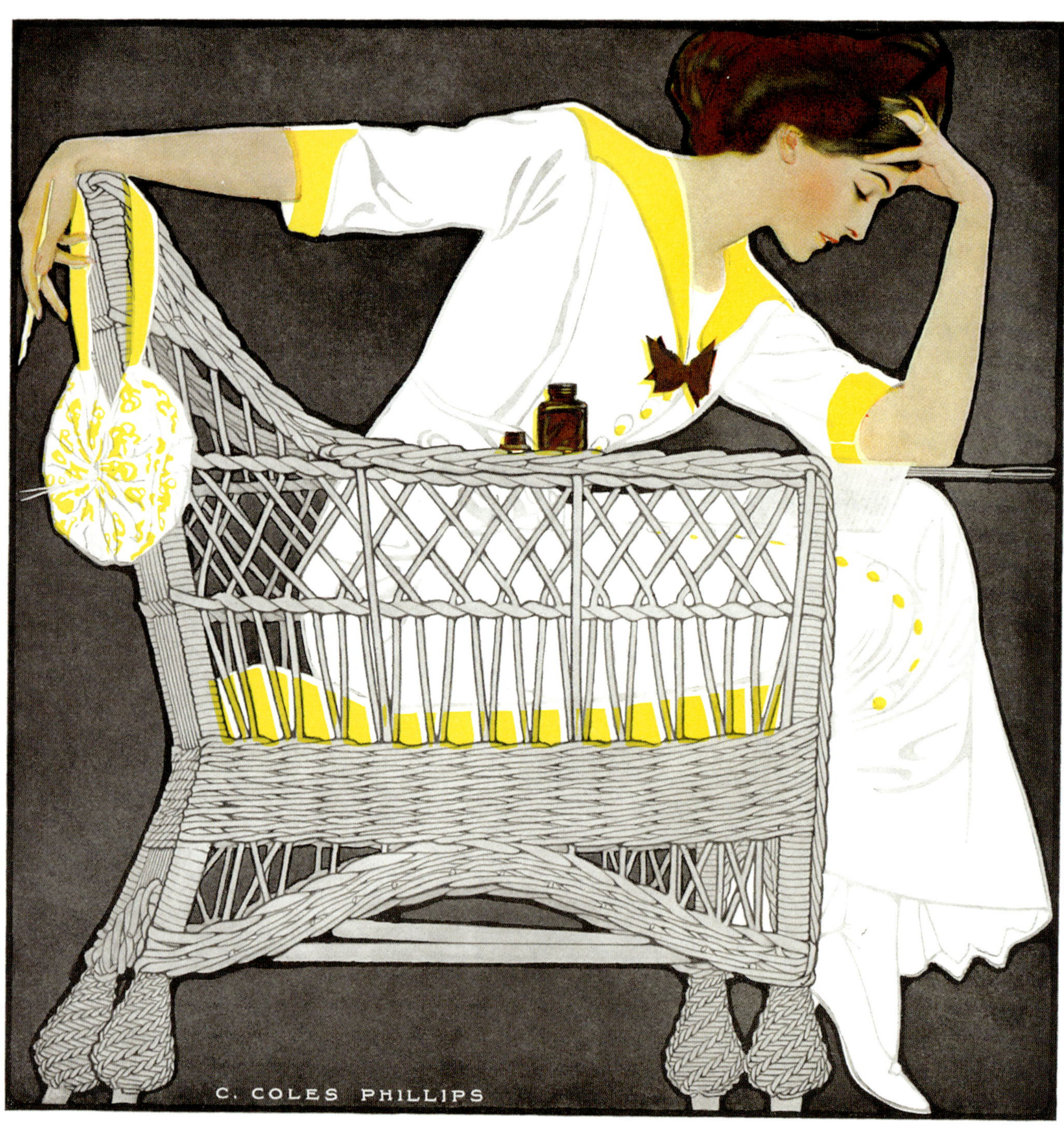

34. *Summer Fiction*
Cover art from *Life* Magazine, September 14, 1911

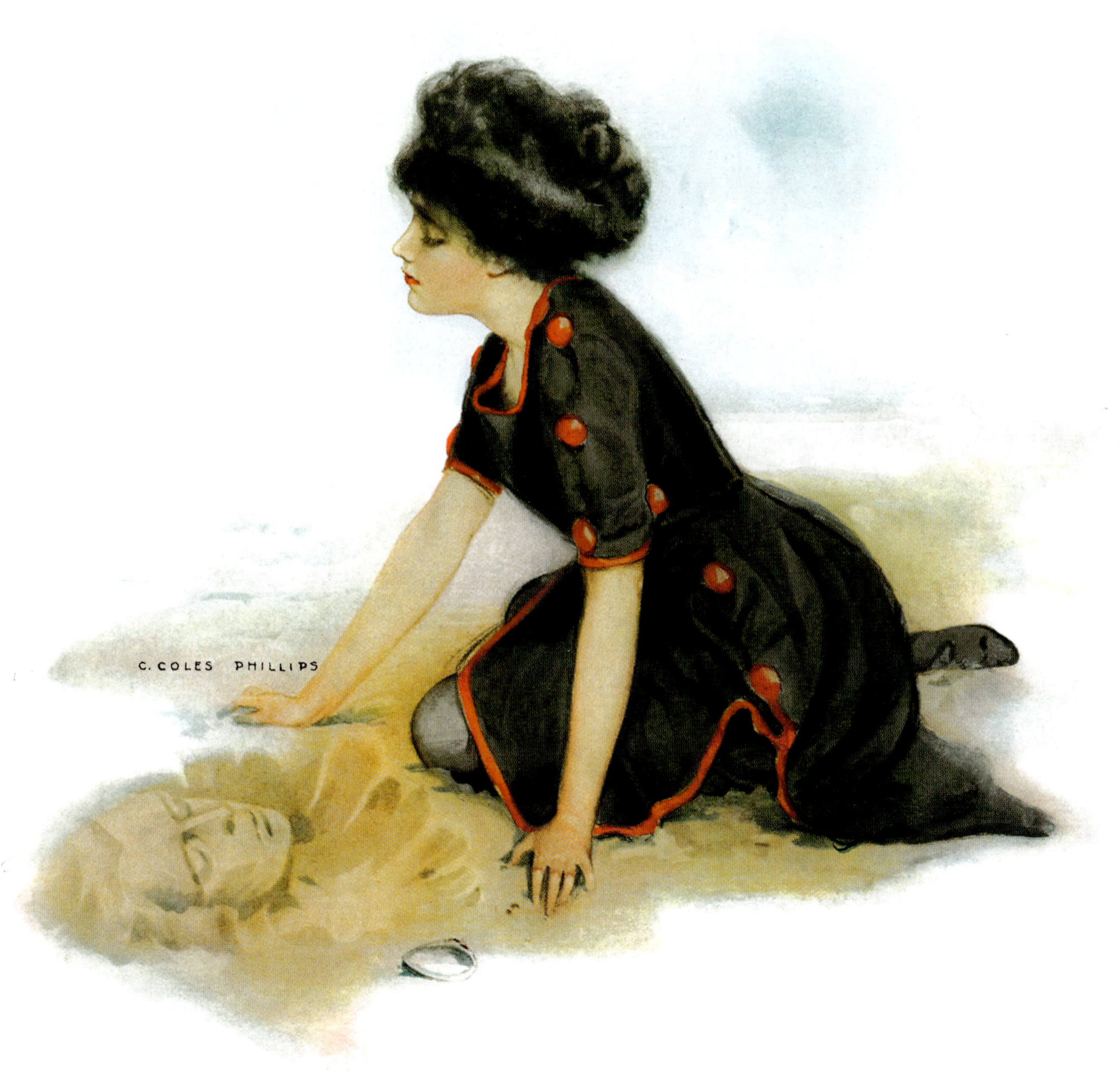

35. *The Sand Man*
Cover art from *Sunday Magazine of the Philadelphia Press*, July 11, 1909

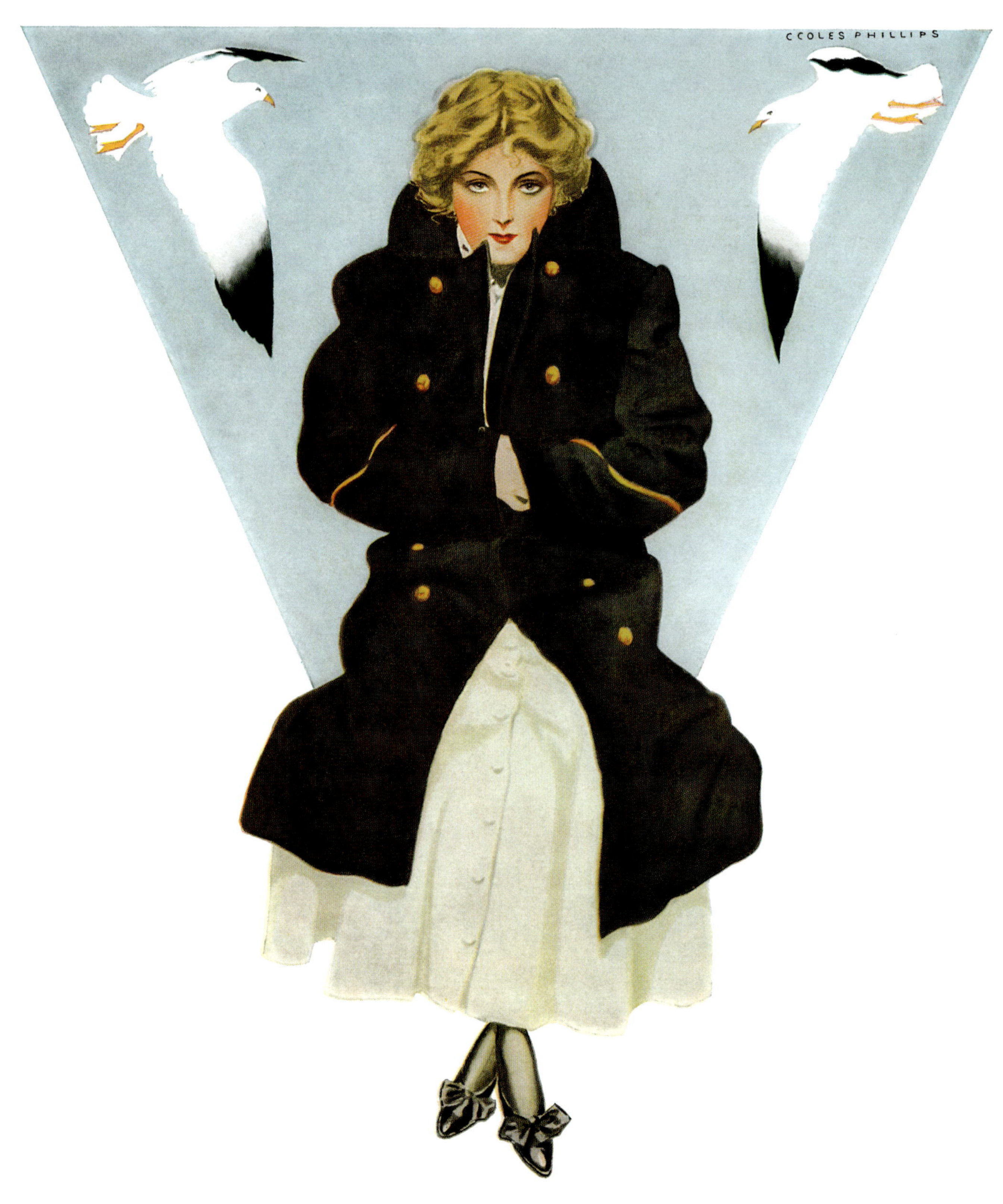

36. *The Midshipmite*
Painted for the United States Naval Academy, 1911

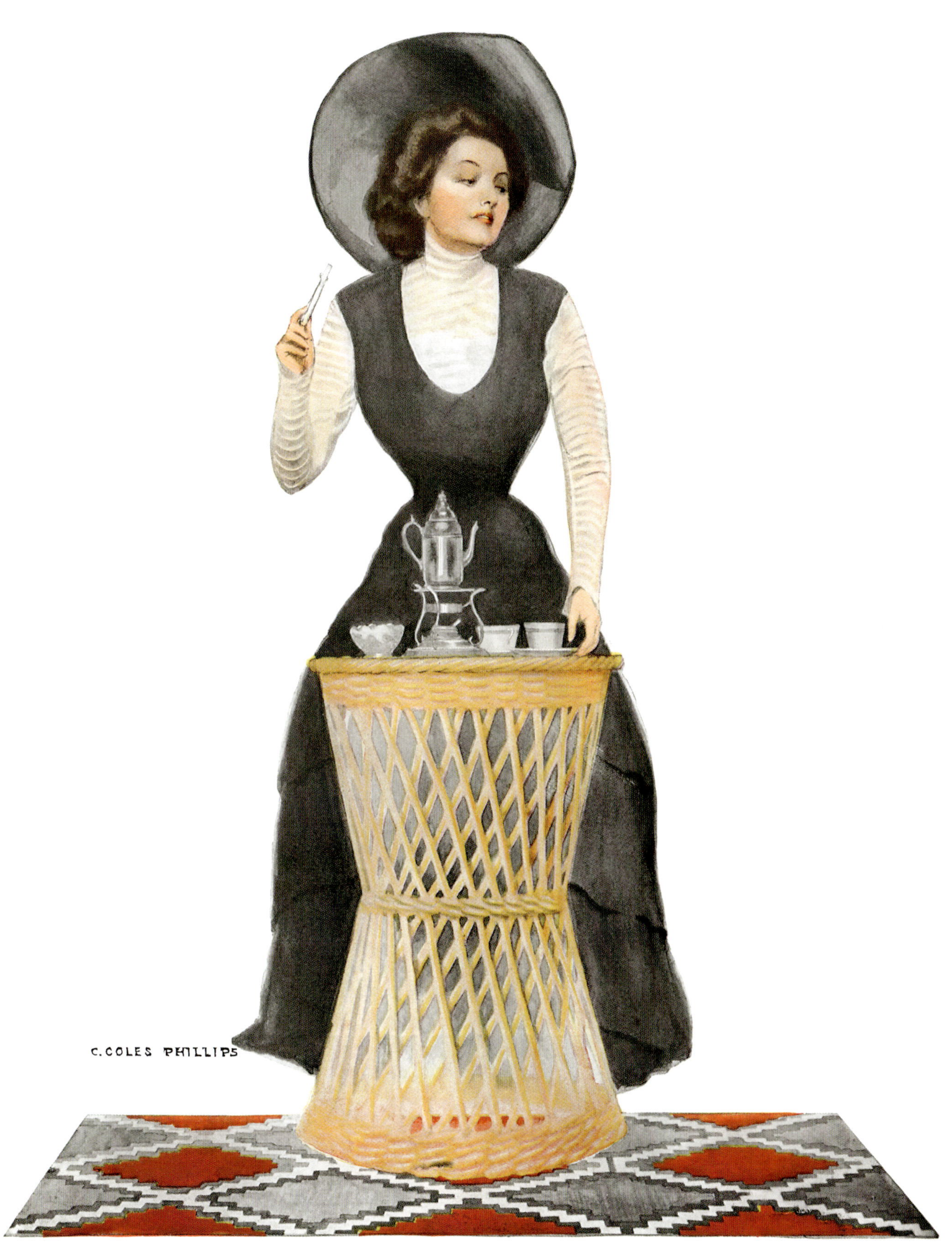

37. *Divine Service*
Cover art from *Life* Magazine, January 28, 1909

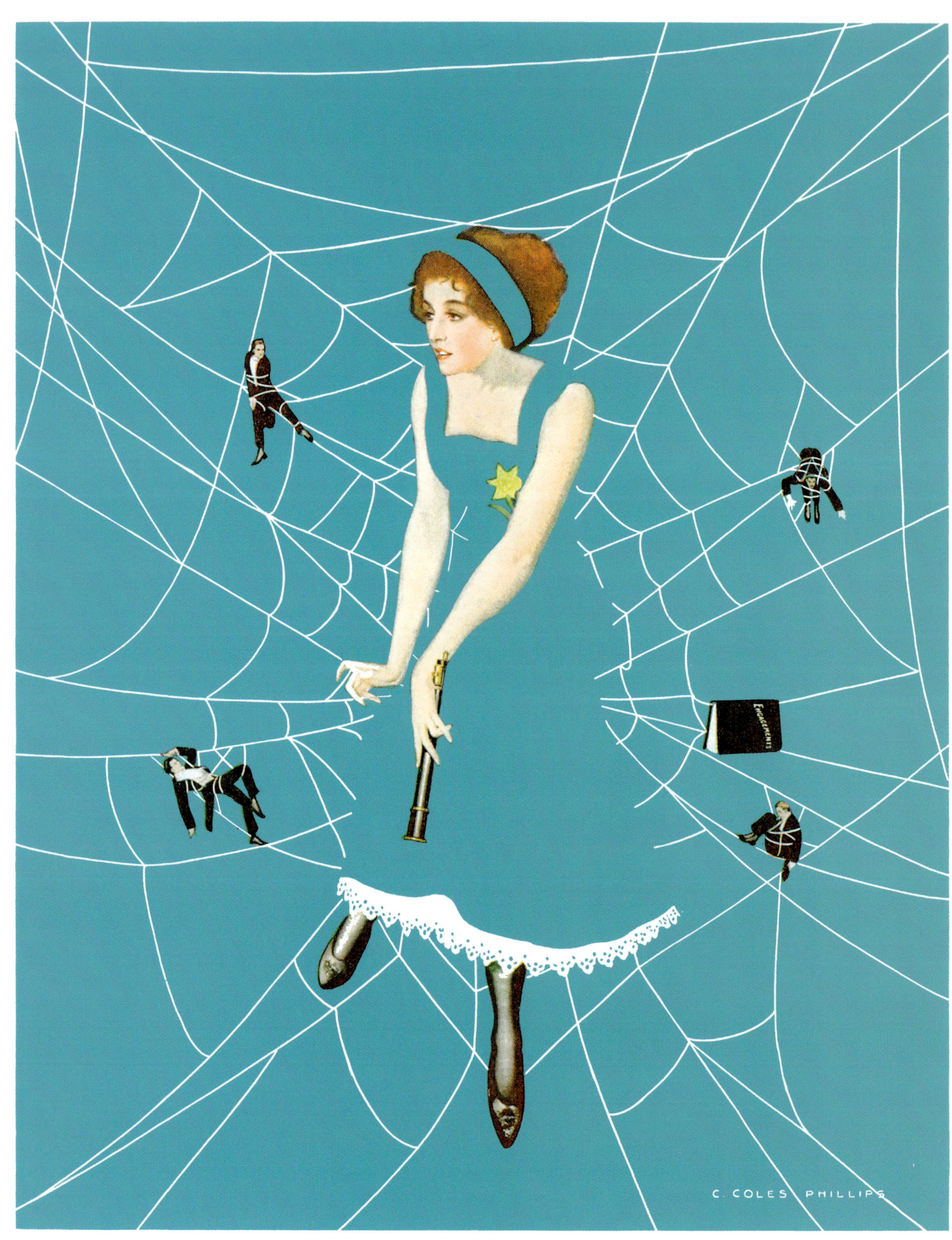

38. *Net Results*
Cover art from *Life* Magazine, August 24, 1911

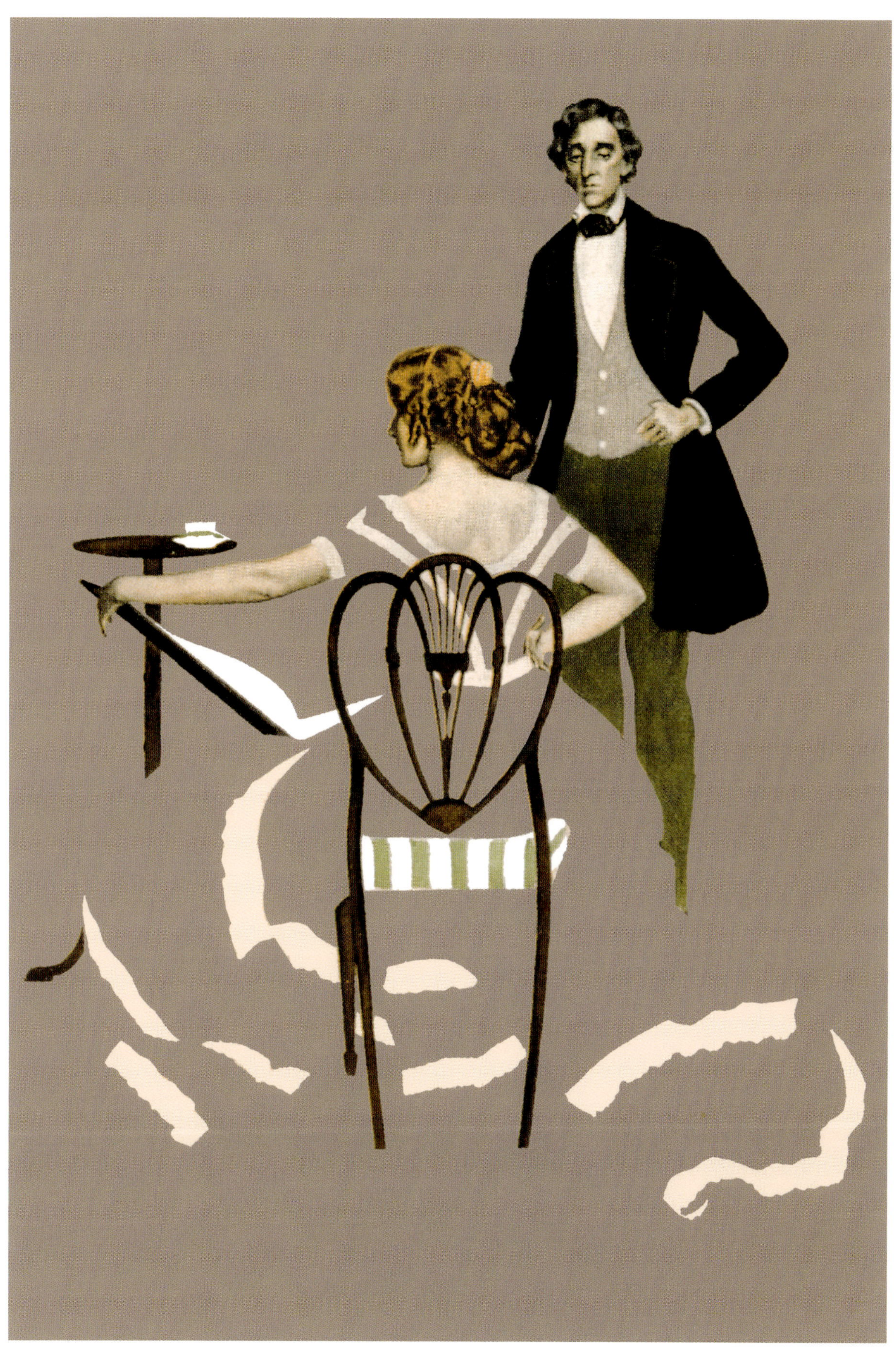

39. *"At this point she became aware that Warner was standing beside her"*
From *The Gorgeous Isle,* 1908

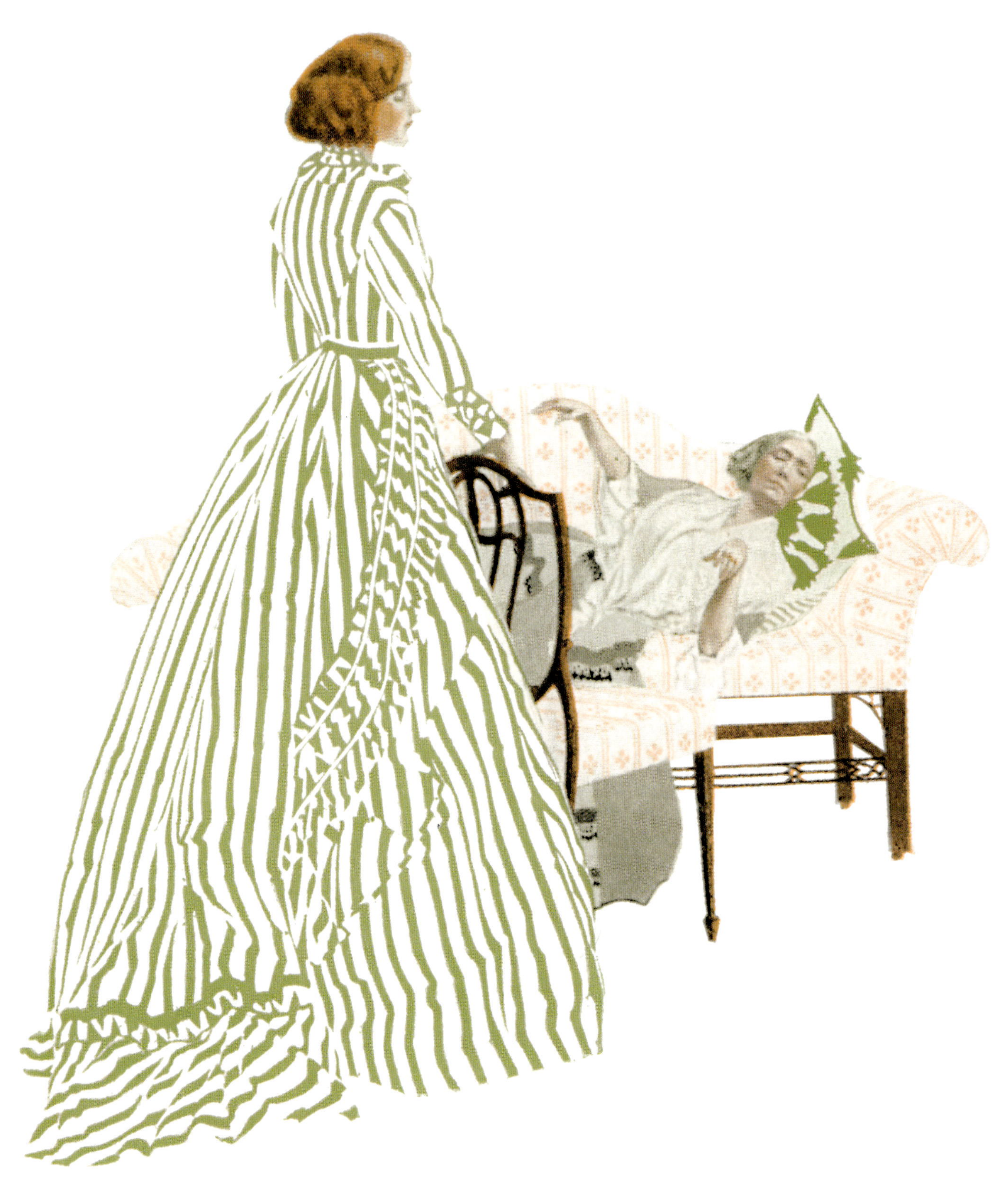

40. *"I never wish to see you again"*
From *The Gorgeous Isle,* 1908

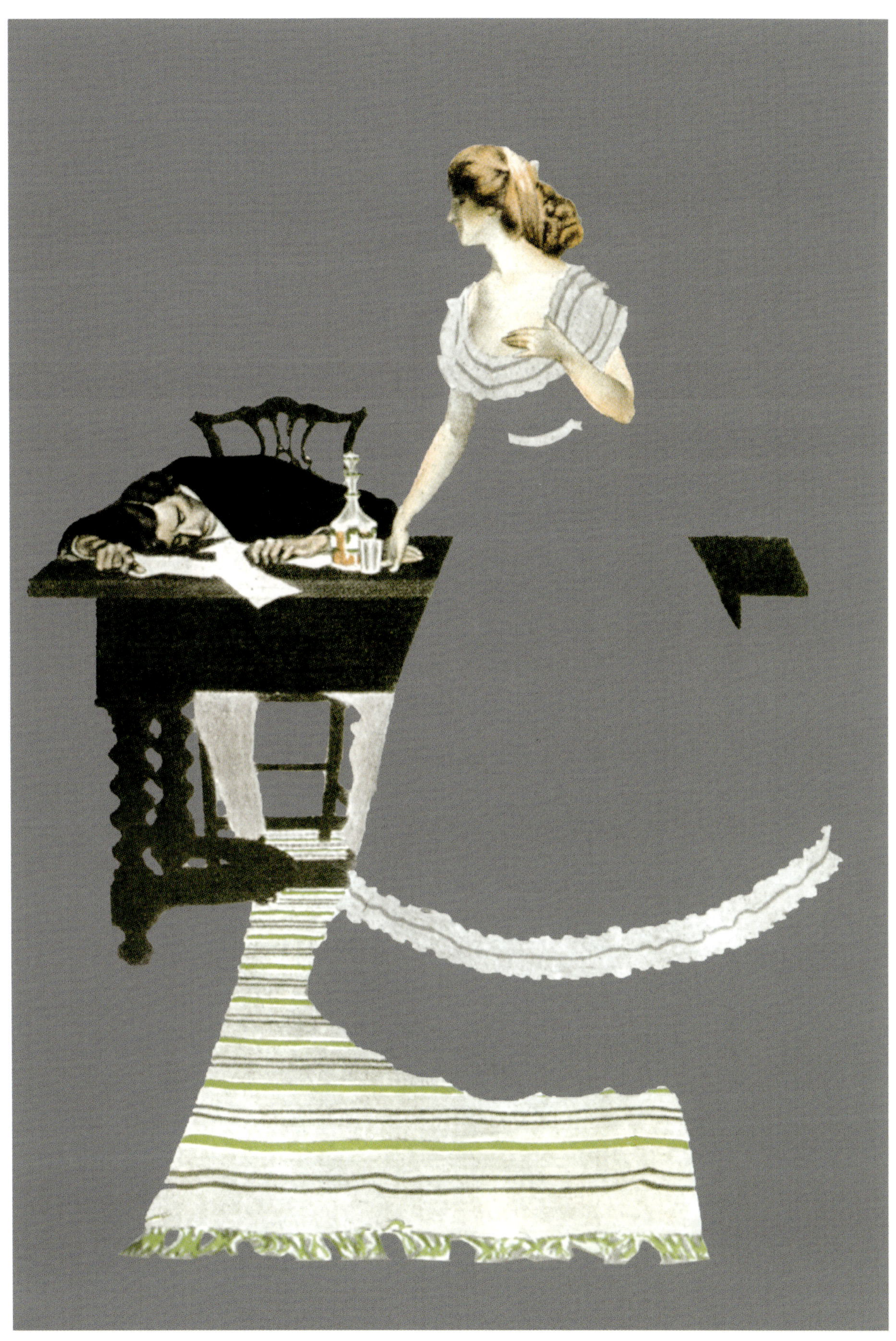

41. *"Then she left the room again"*
From *The Gorgeous Isle,* 1908

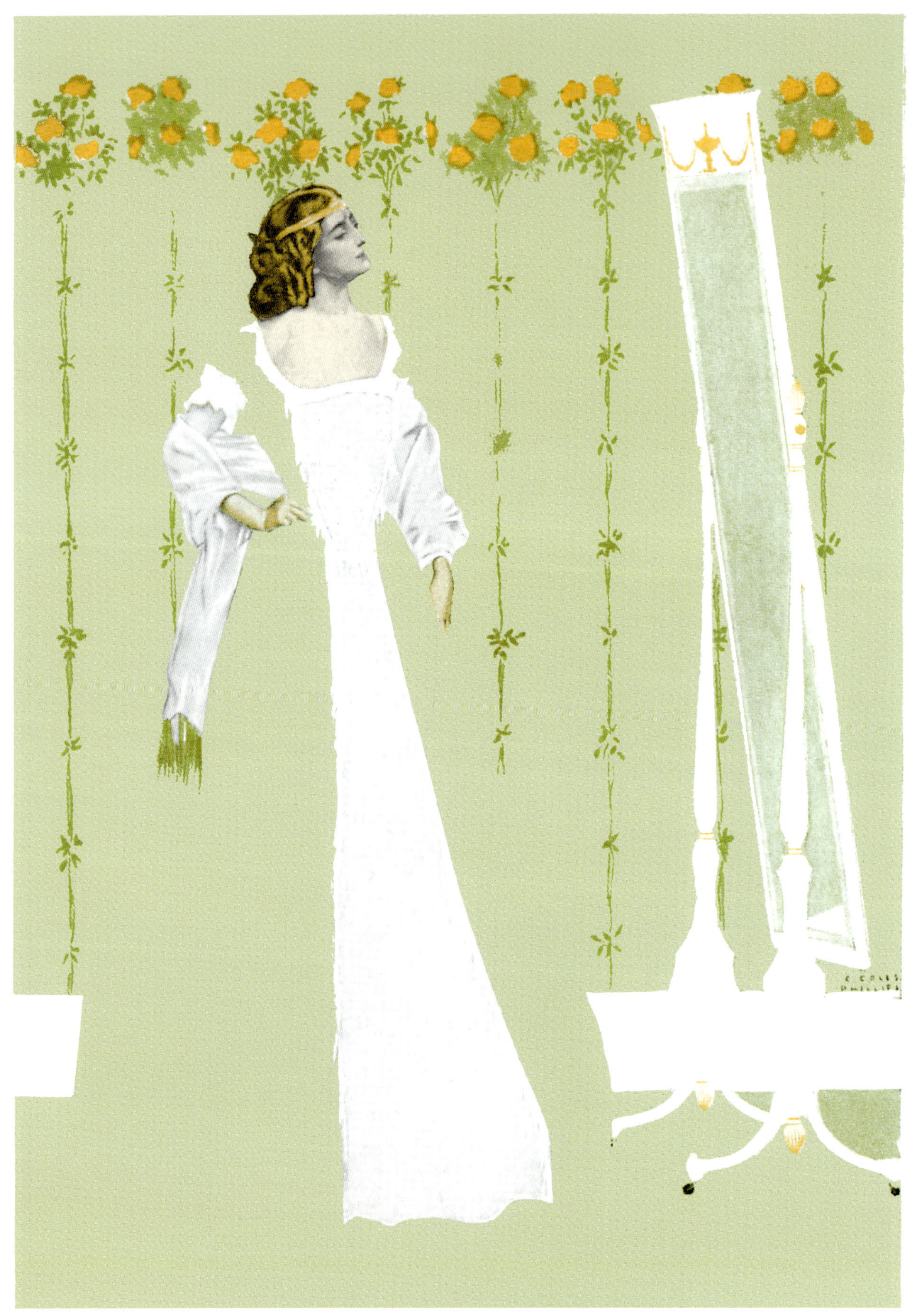

42. *"But what a joy to see you in color. How does it happen?"*
From *The Gorgeous Isle,* 1908

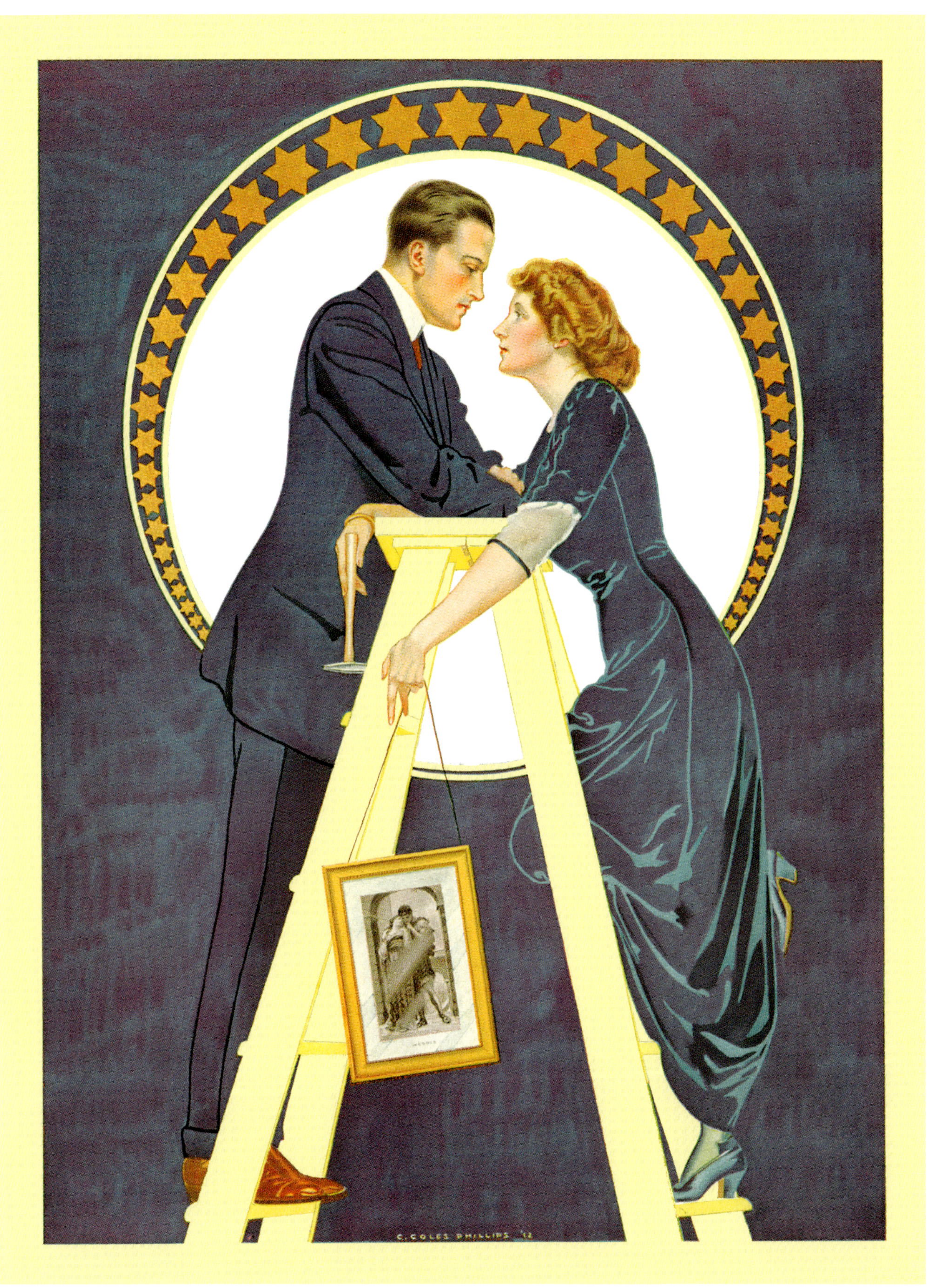

43. *Hanging Pictures*
Bobbs-Merrill Co., 1912

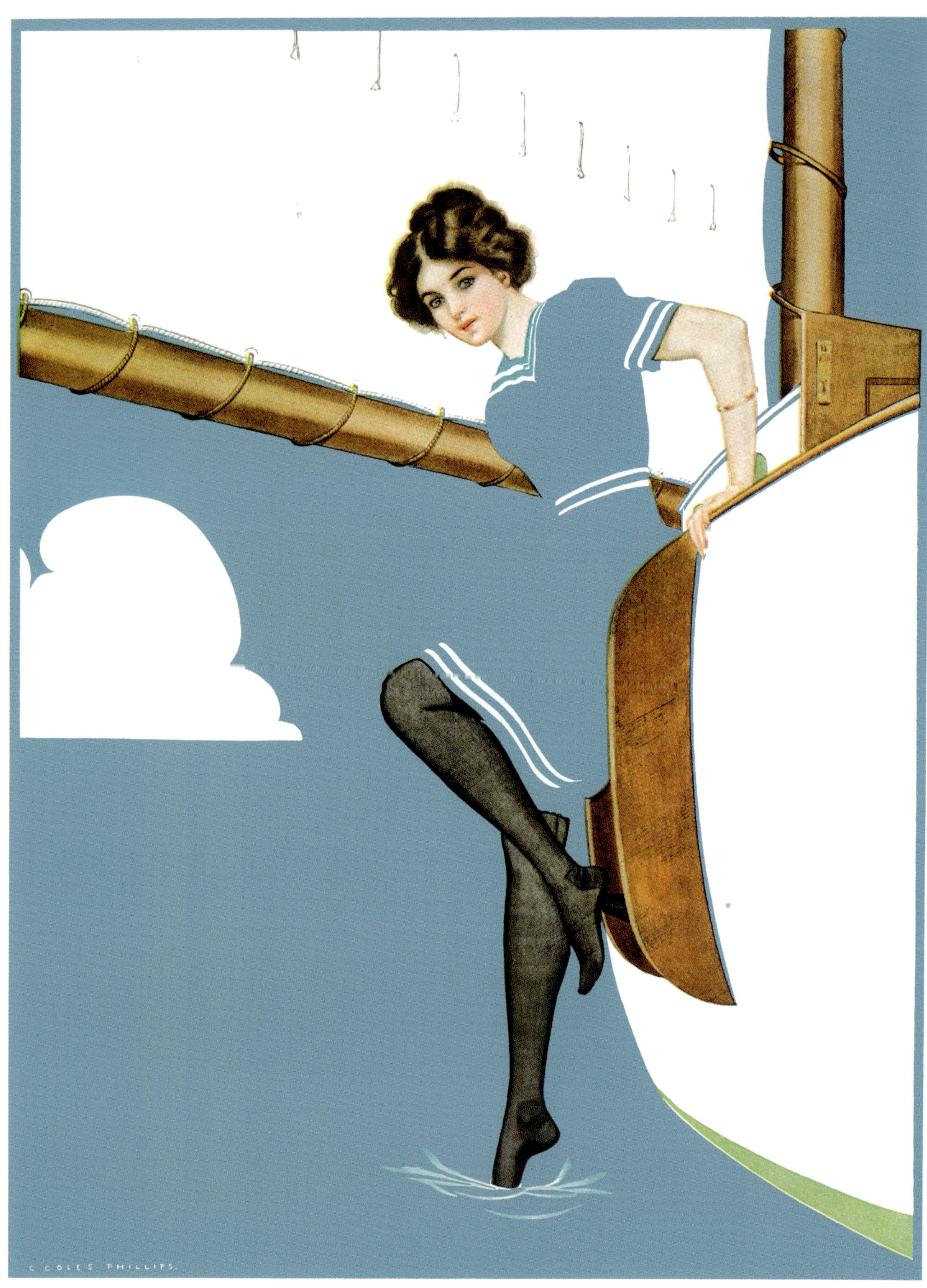

44. *Toes in the Water*
Bobbs-Merrill Co., 1912

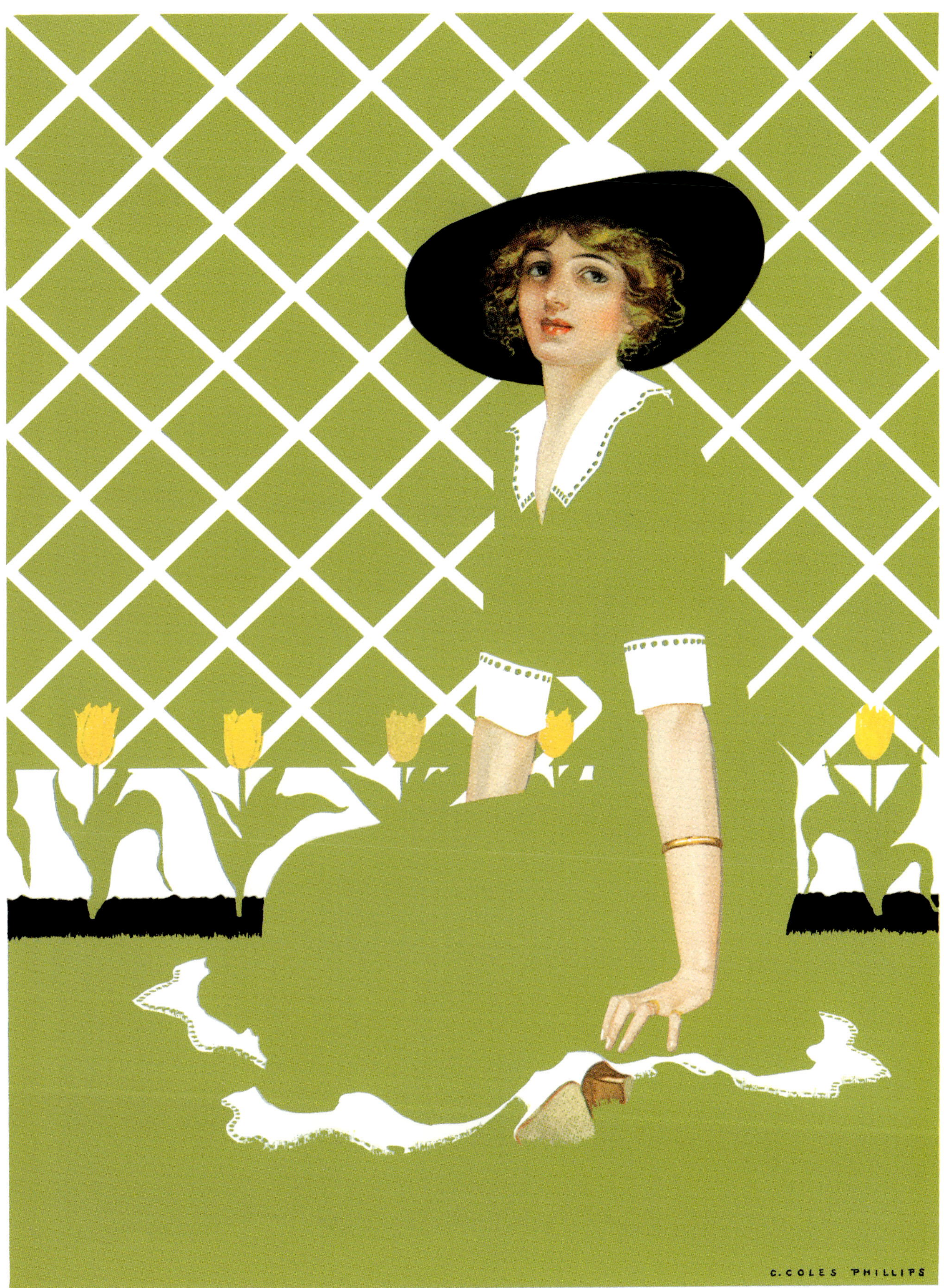

45. *Tulips in the Garden*
Bobbs-Merrill Co., 1912

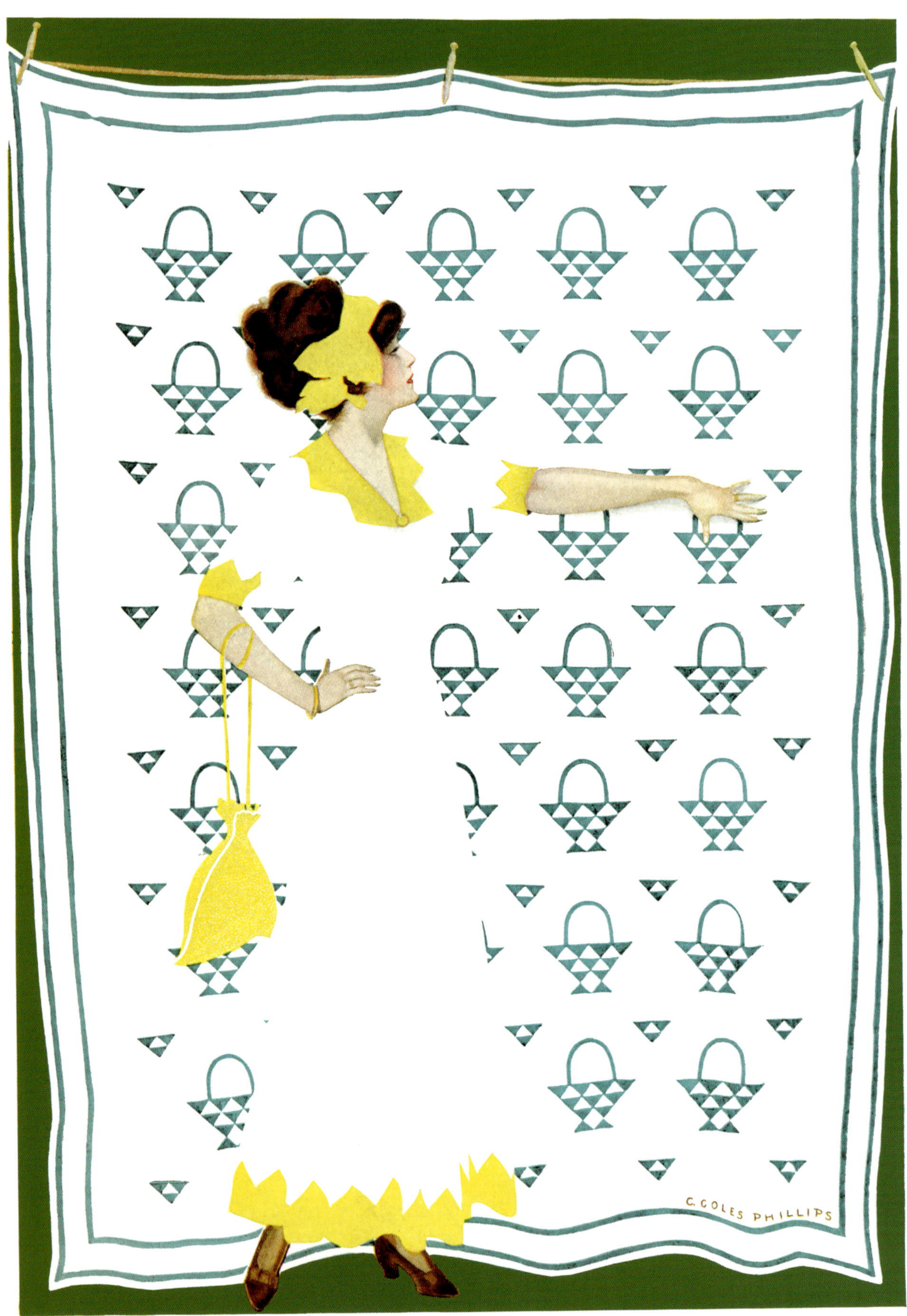

46. *The Winning Quilt*
Bobbs-Merrill Co., 1912

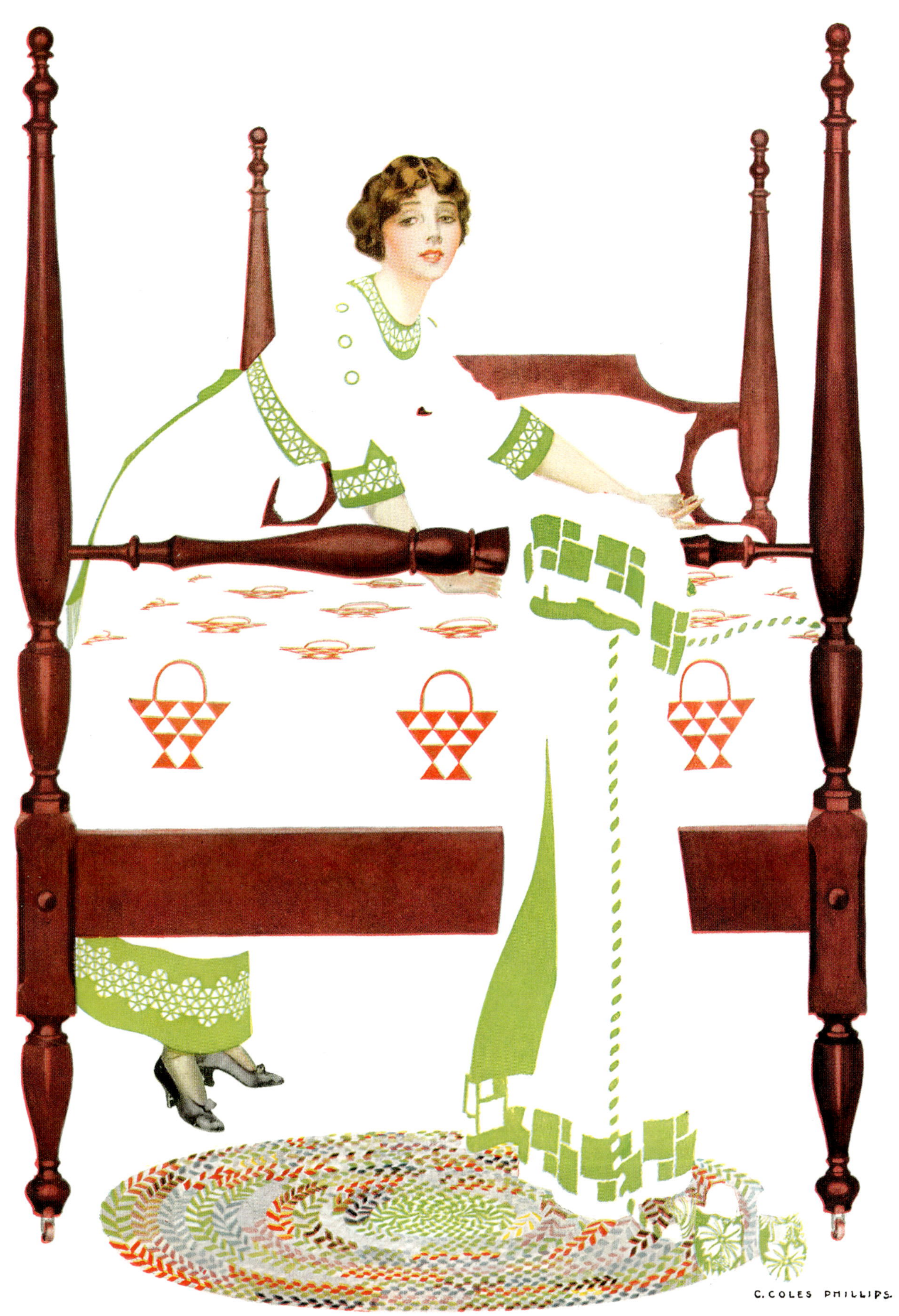

47. *The Four-Poster*
Bobbs-Merrill Co., 1912

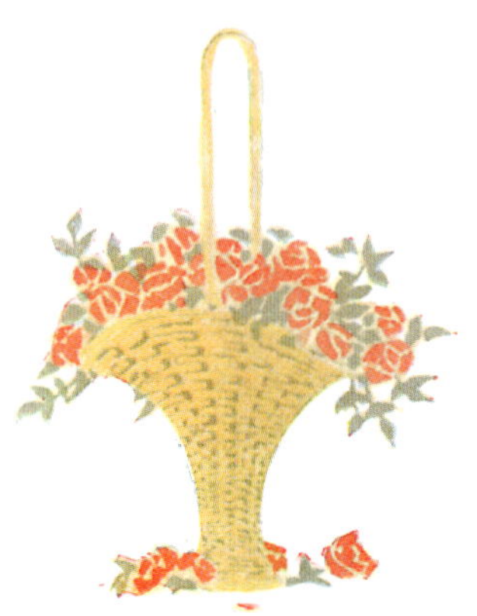

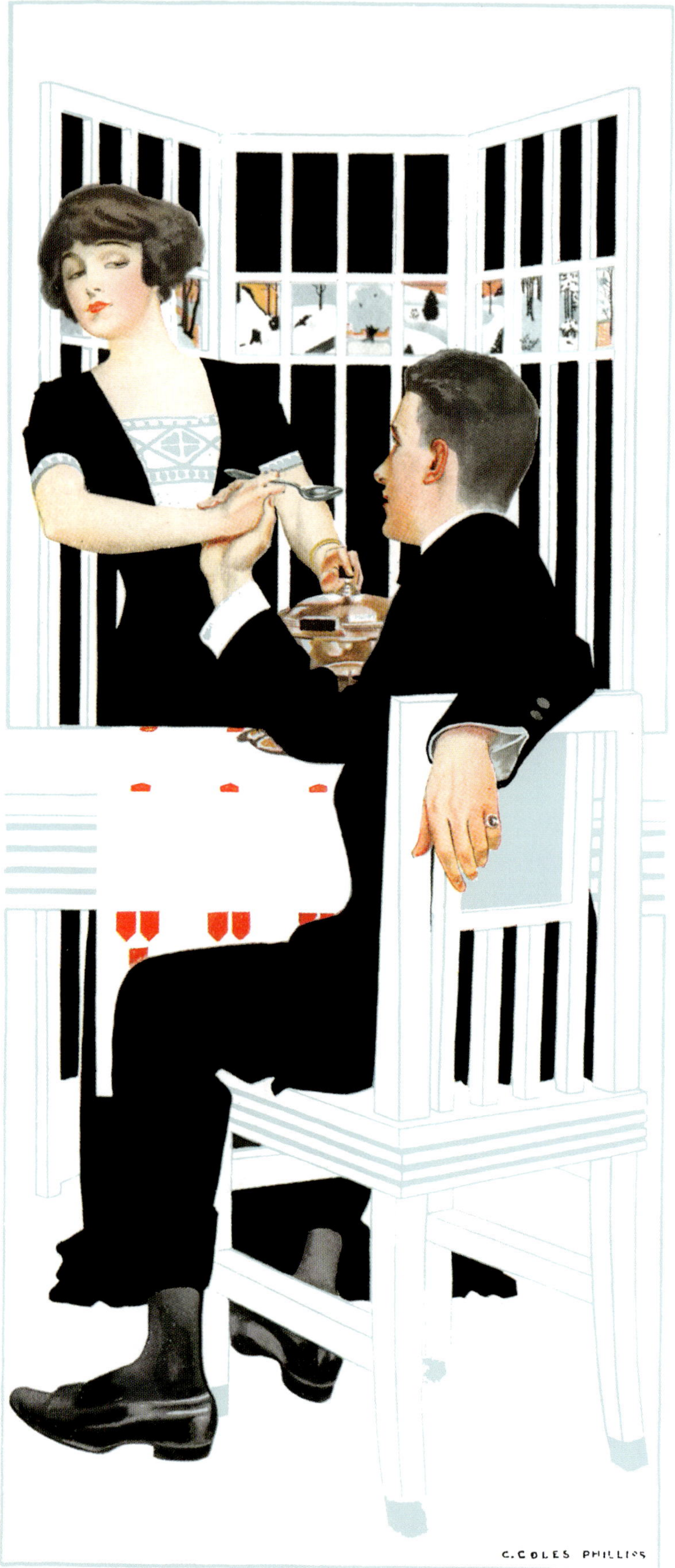

C.COLES PHILLIPS

48. *Taking Your Medicine*
Bobbs-Merrill Co., 1912

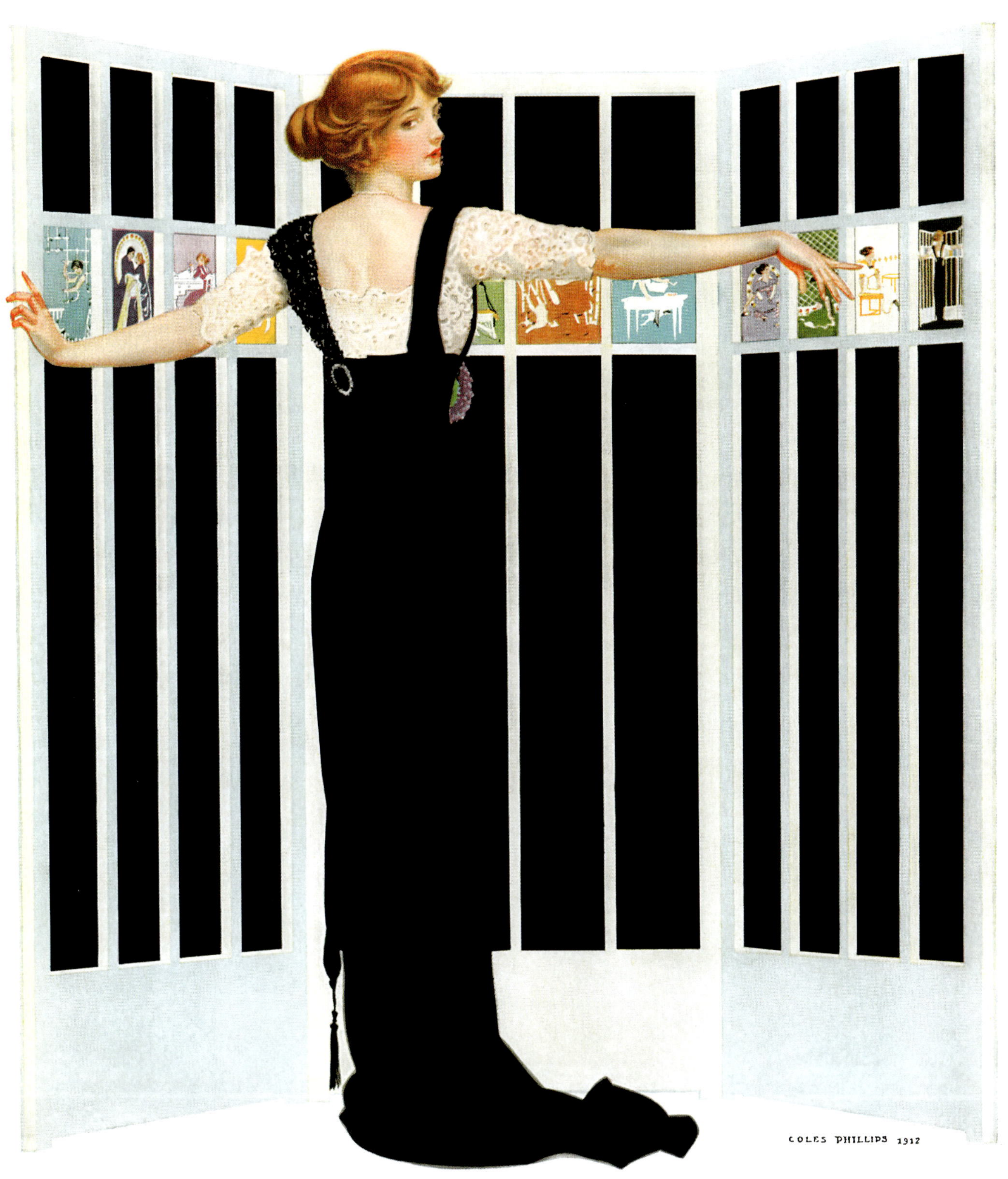

49. *In the Gallery*
Bobbs-Merrill Co., 1912

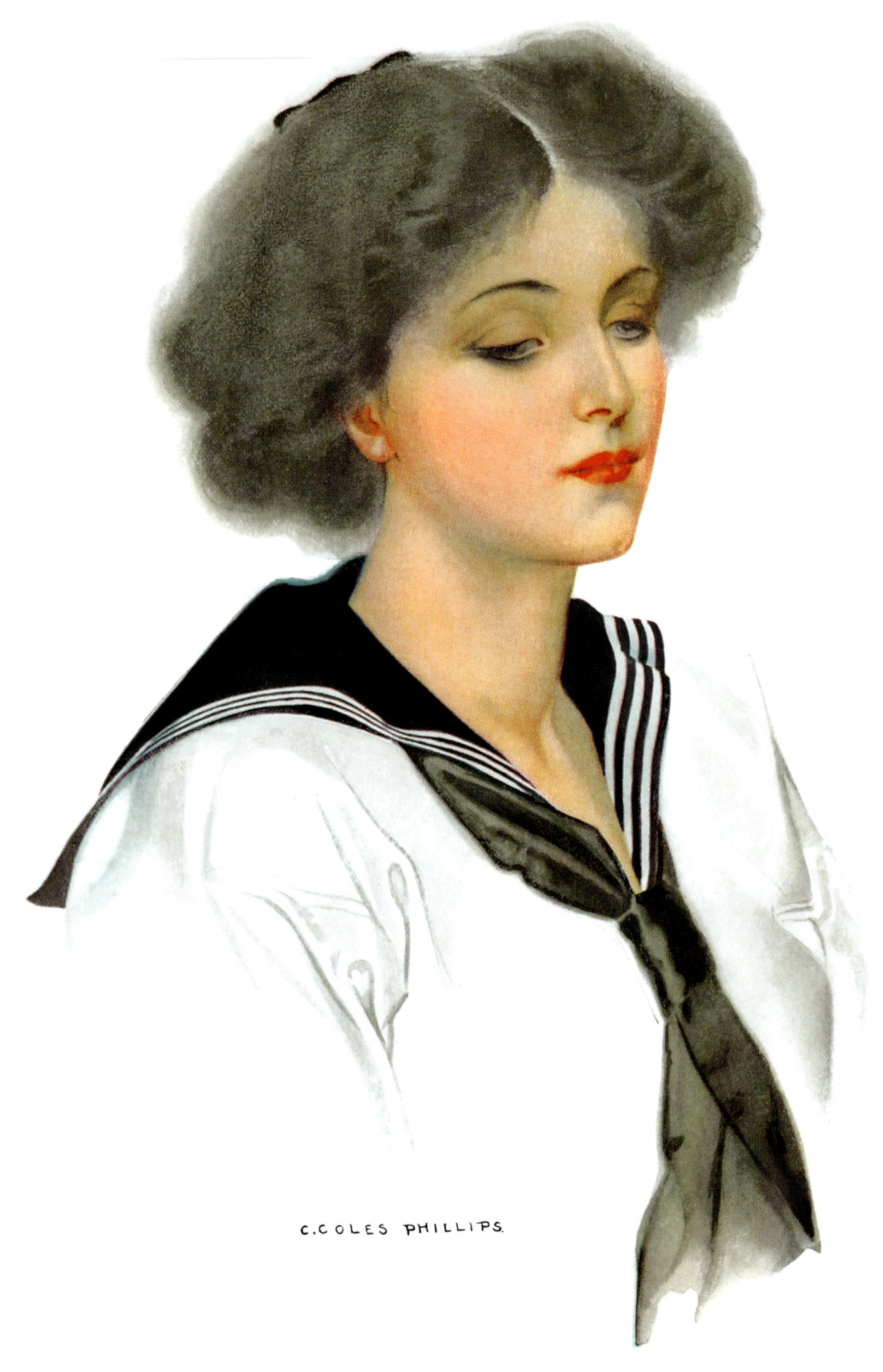

50. *Off to Sea*
Bobbs-Merrill Co., 1912

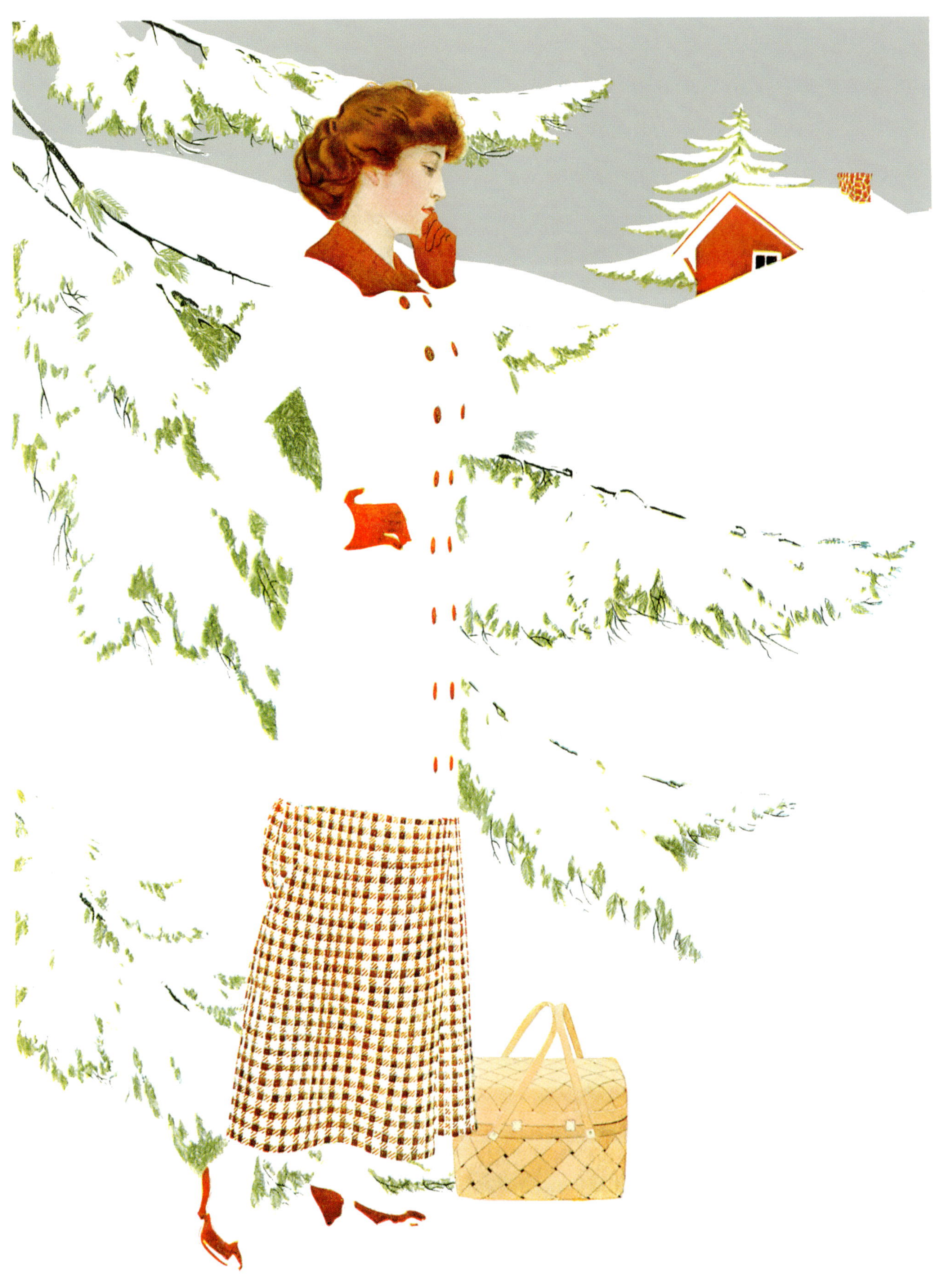

51. *A Christmas Visit*
Bobbs-Merrill Co., 1912

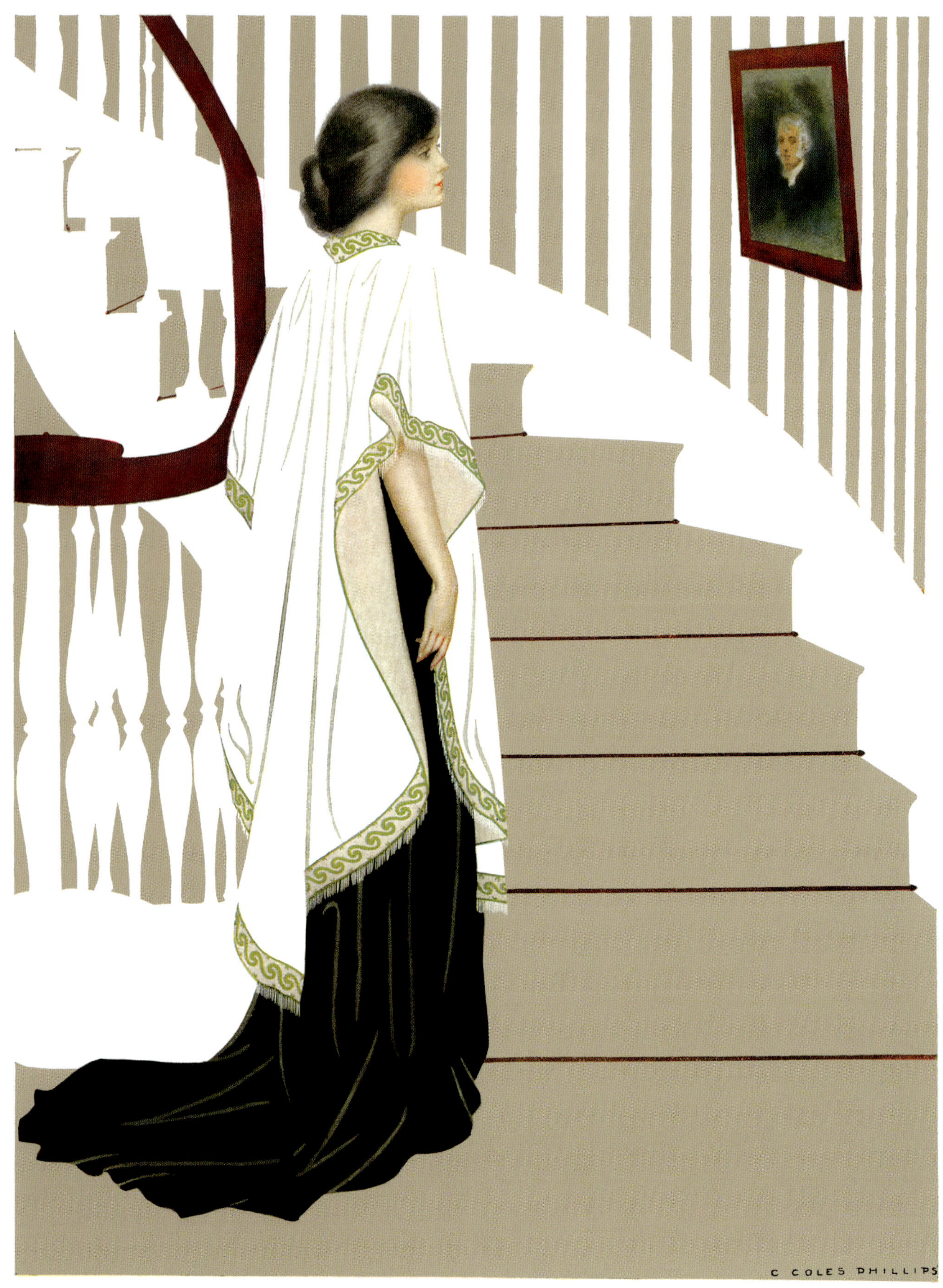

52. *The Stairwell*
Bobbs-Merrill Co., 1912

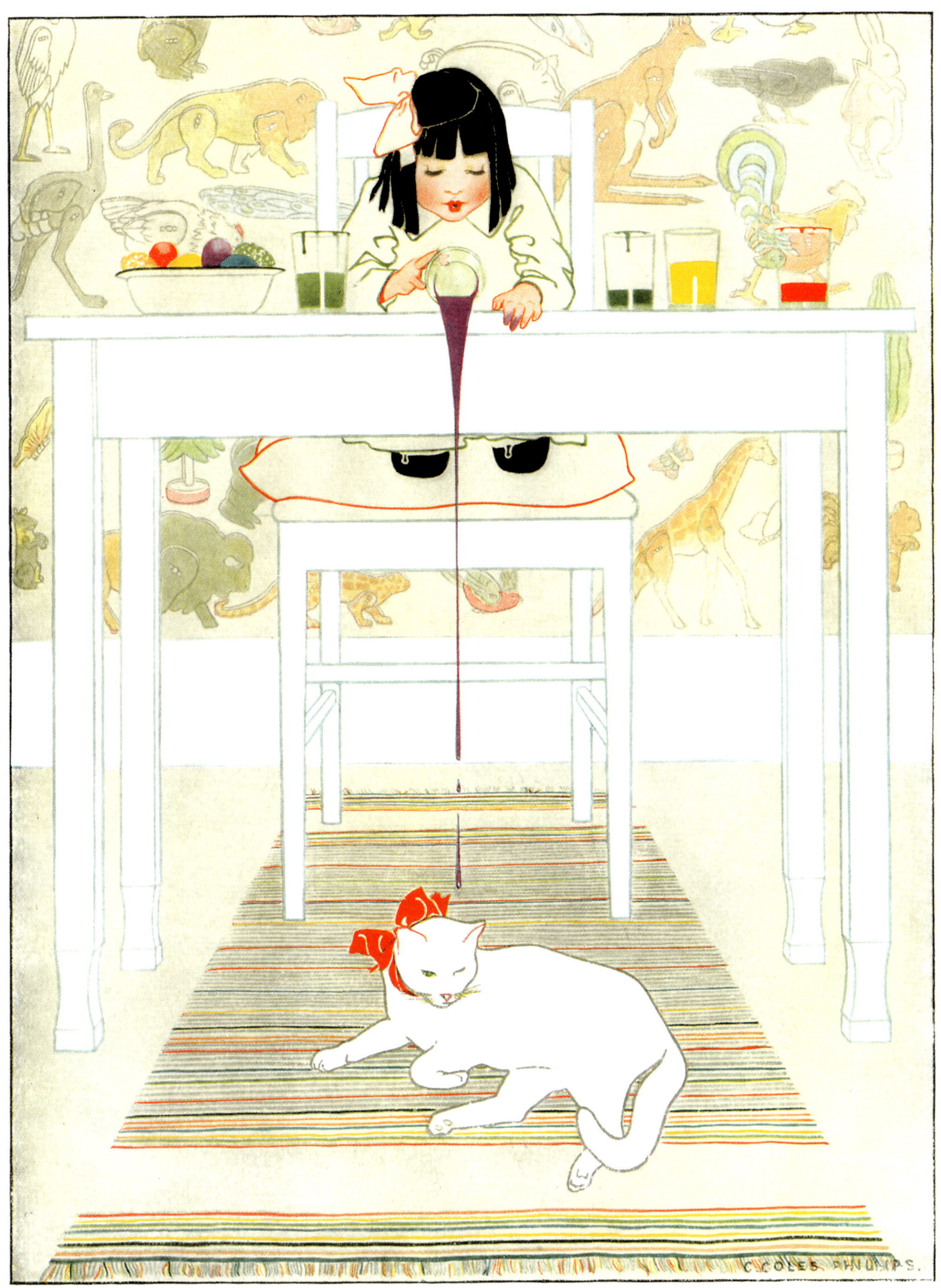

53. *At the Table*
Bobbs-Merrill Co., 1912

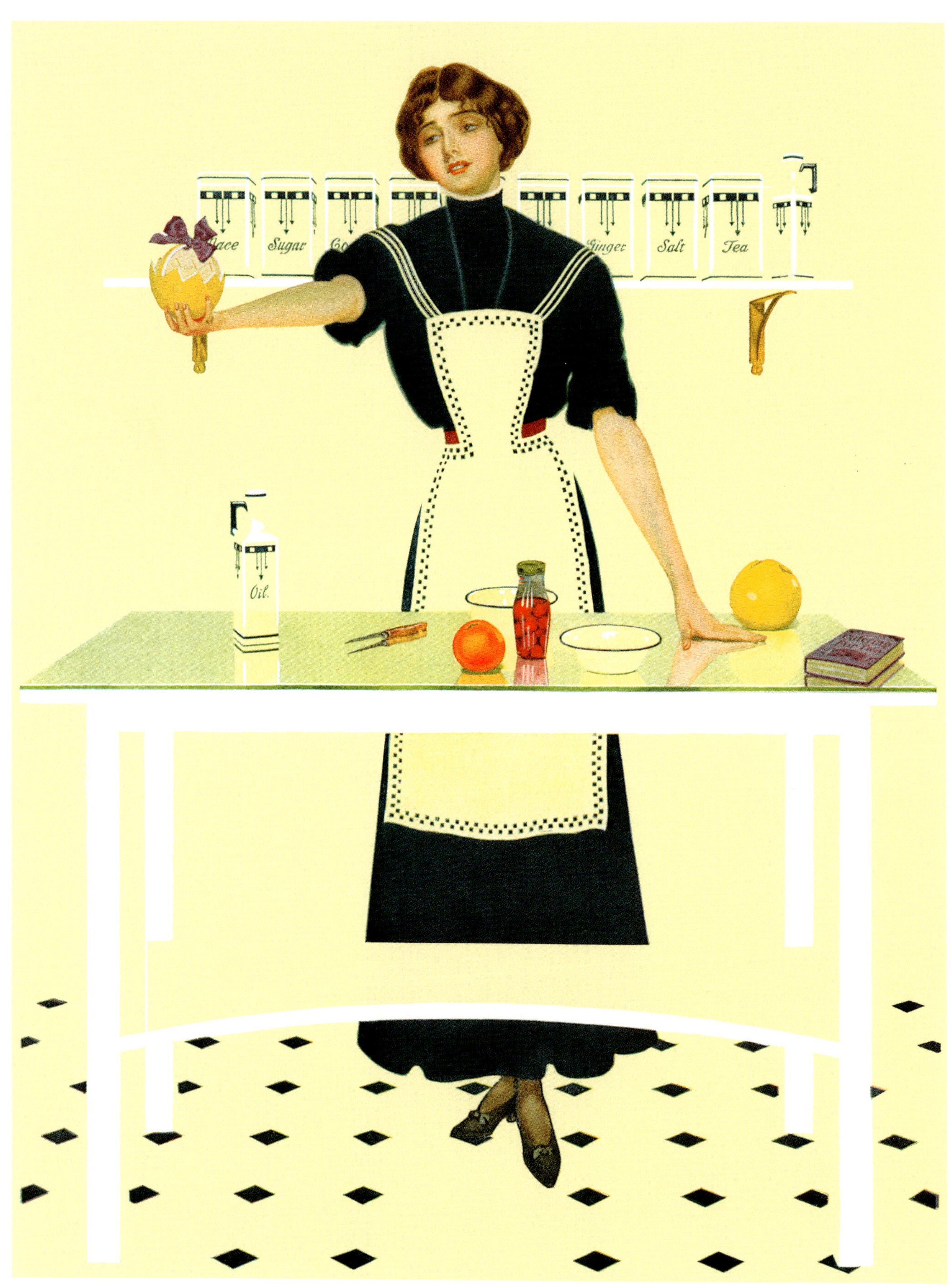

54. *A Perfect Cut*
Bobbs-Merrill Co., 1912

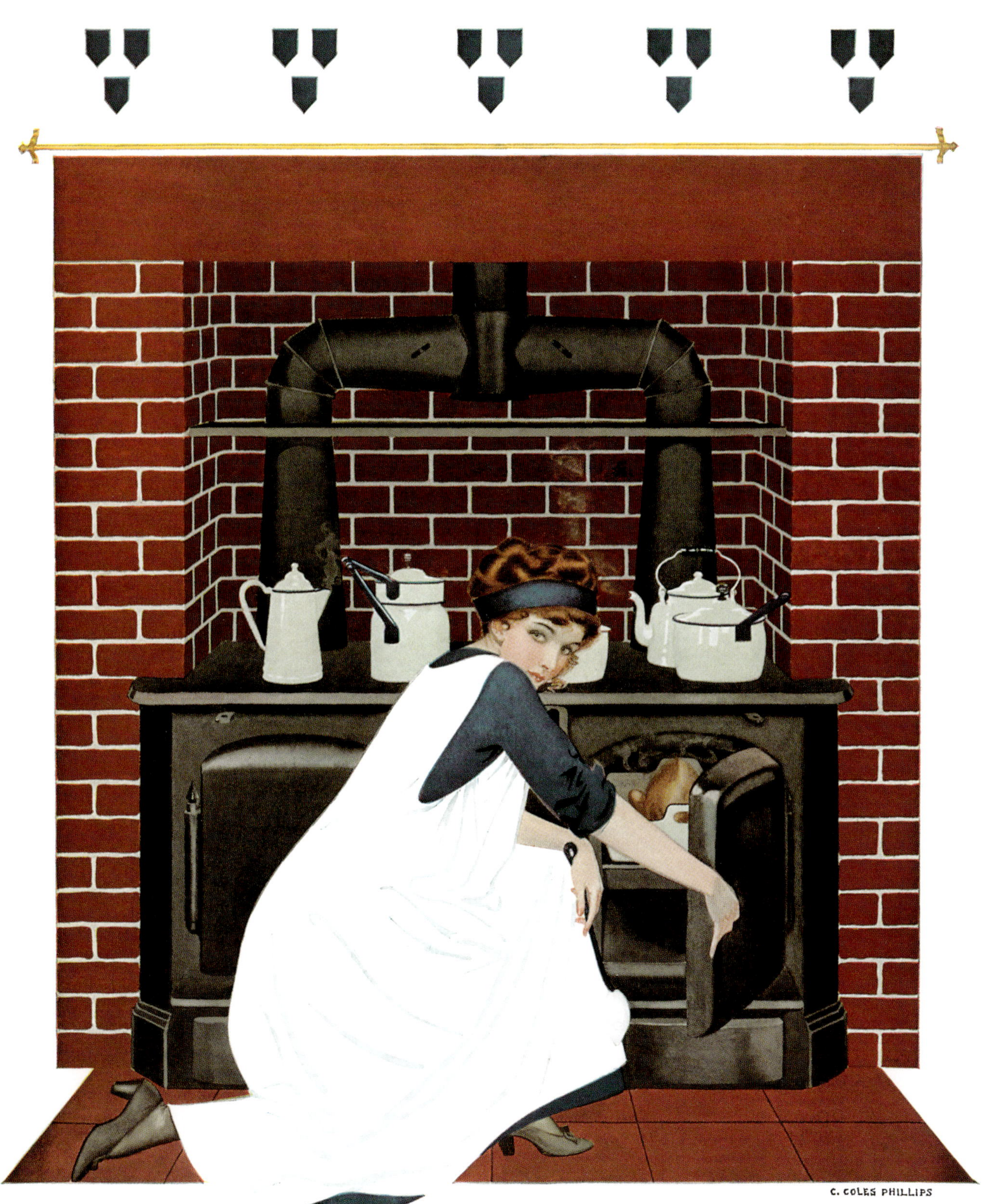

55. *Roasting the Turkey*
Bobbs-Merrill Co., 1912

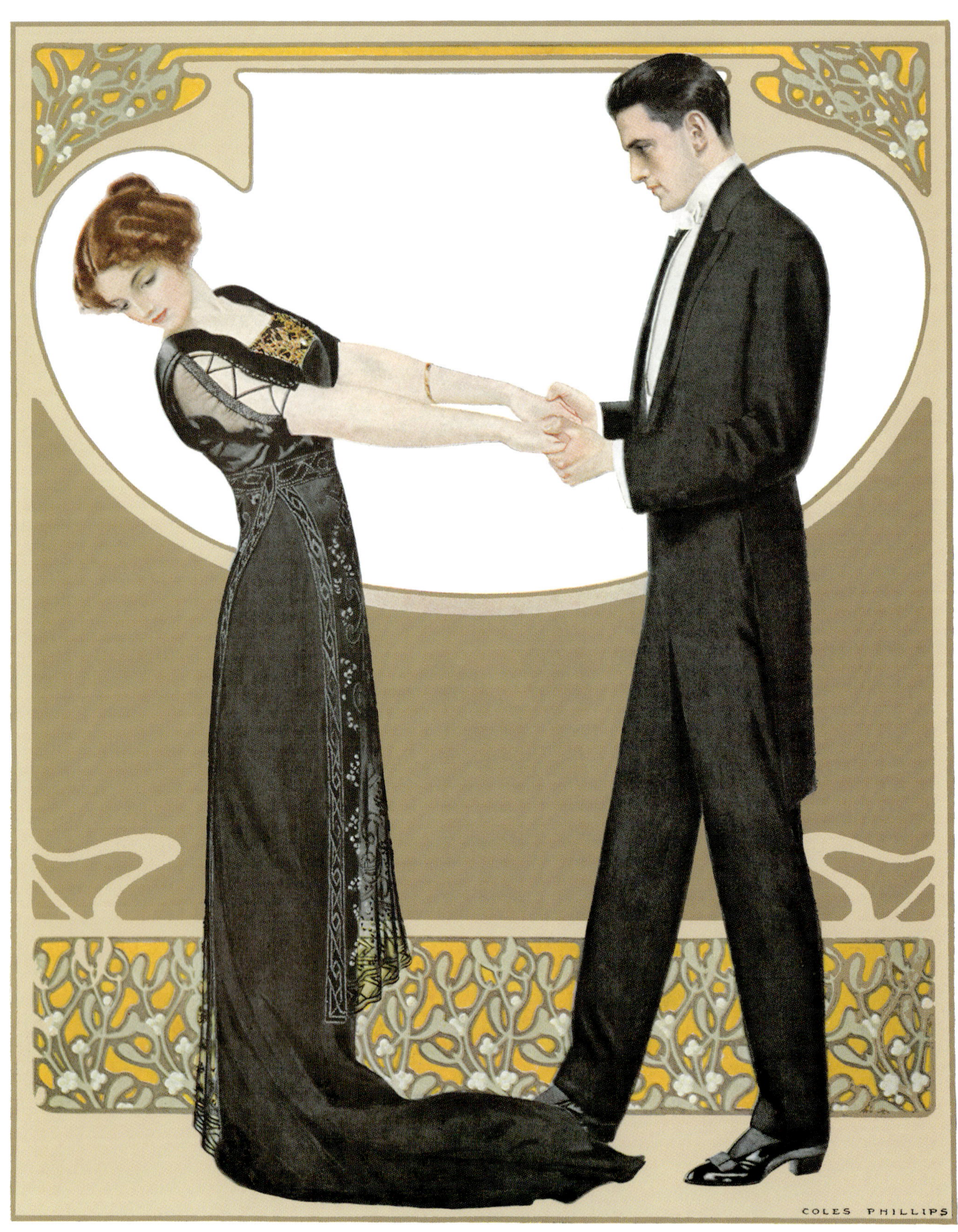

56. *The Couple*
Bobbs-Merrill Co., 1912

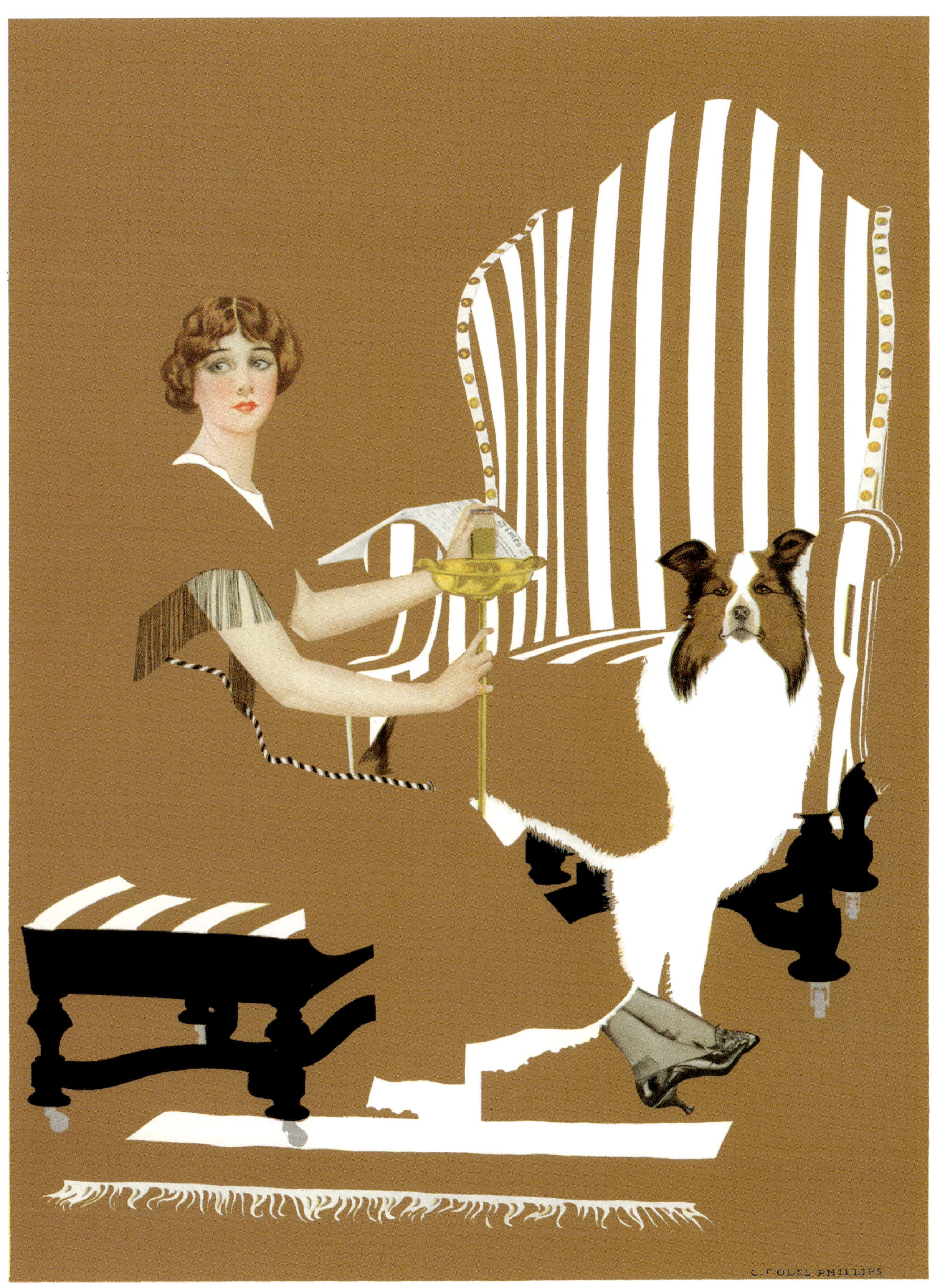

57. *A Striking Match*
Bobbs-Merrill Co., 1912

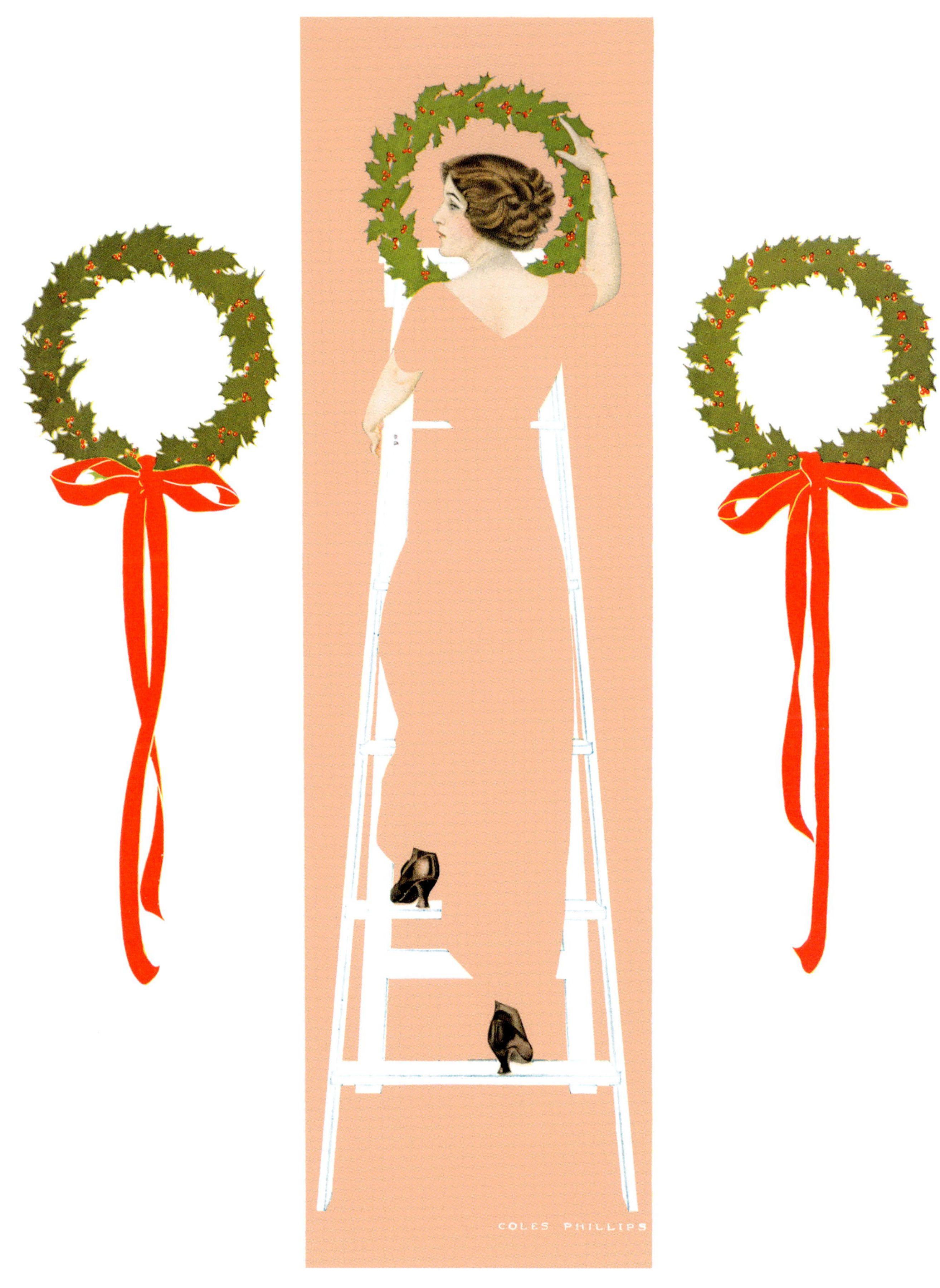

58. *Hanging Wreaths*
From *Life* Magazine, 1912

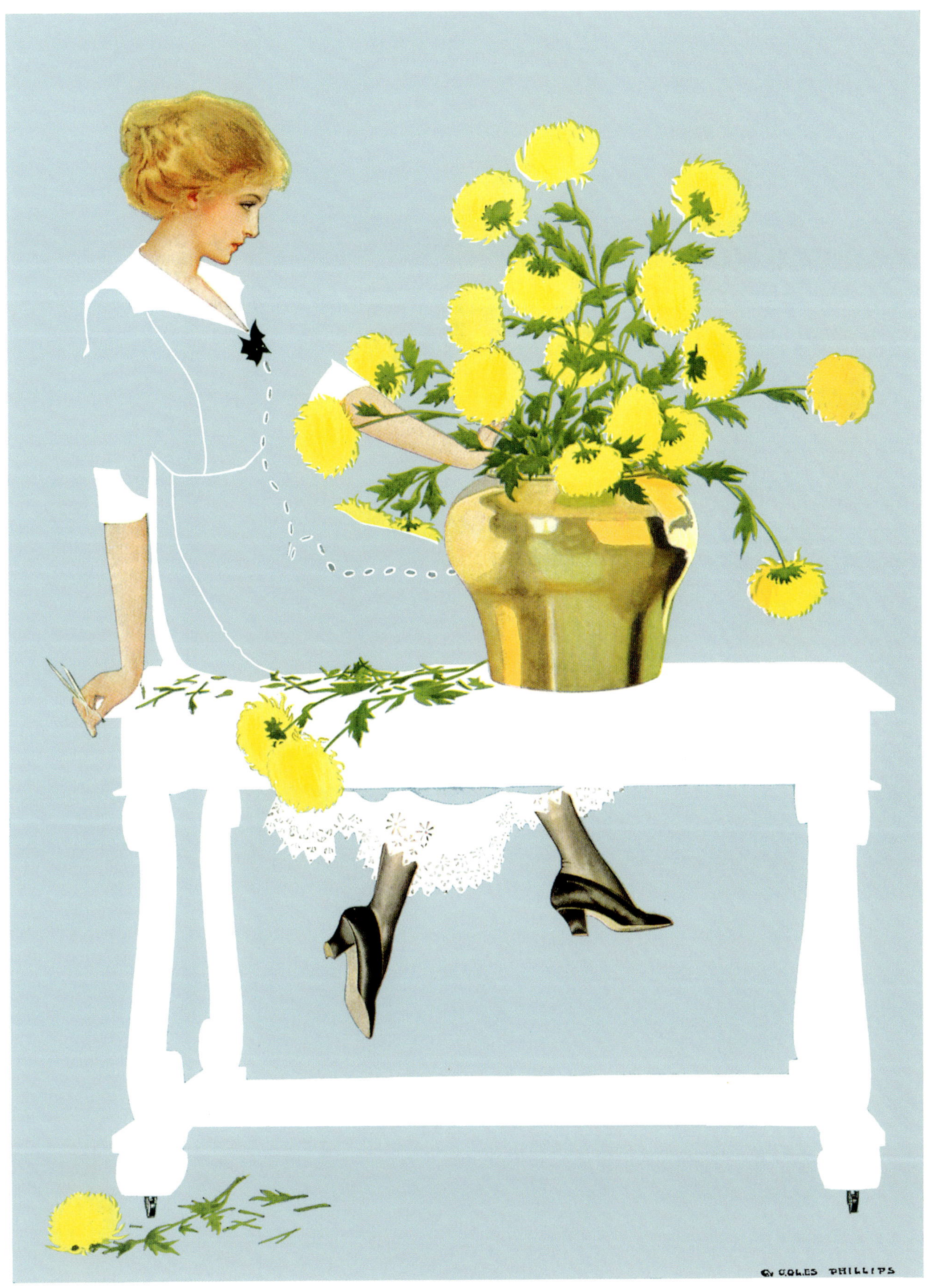

59. *Shaping the Bouquet*
Bobbs-Merrill Co., 1912

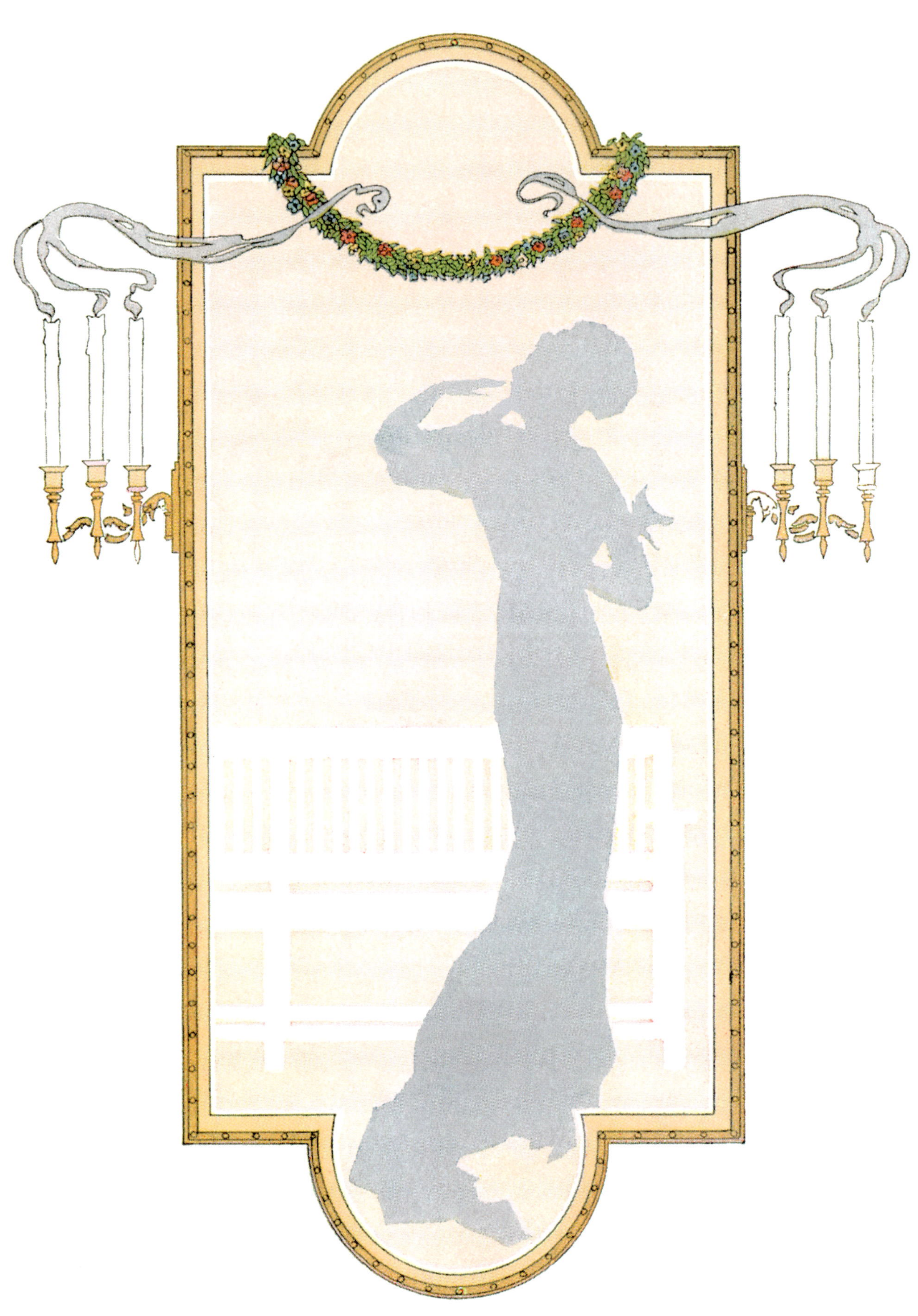

60. *Title Page Art, A Young Man's Fancy*
Bobbs-Merrill Co., 1912

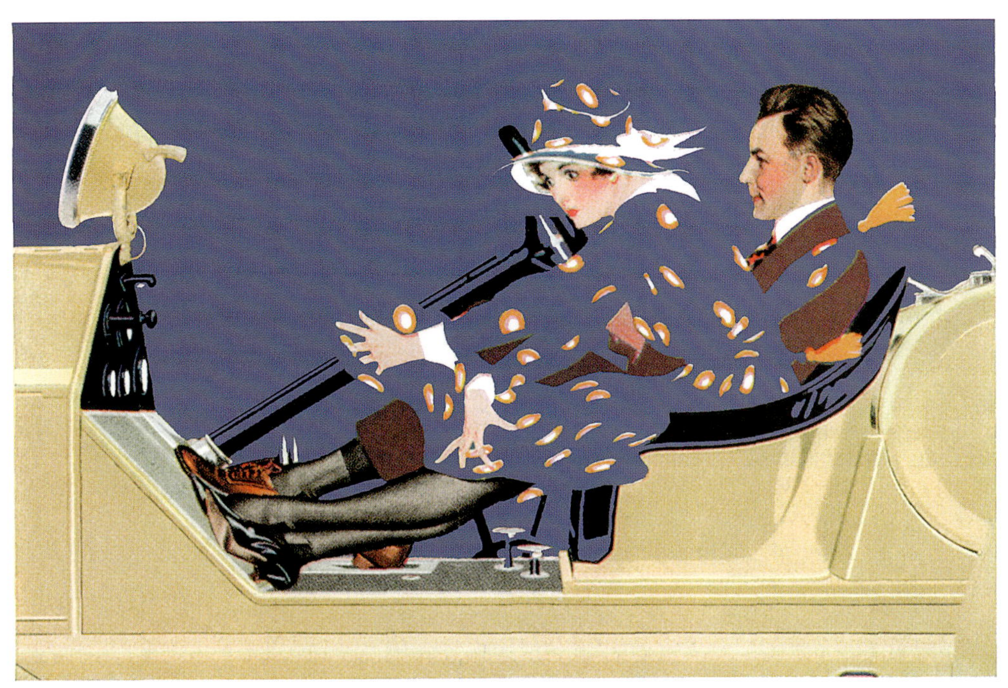

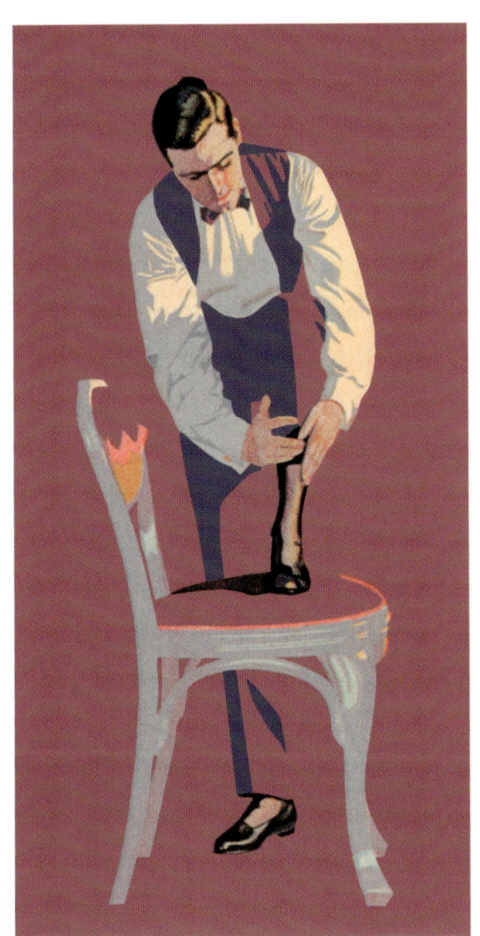

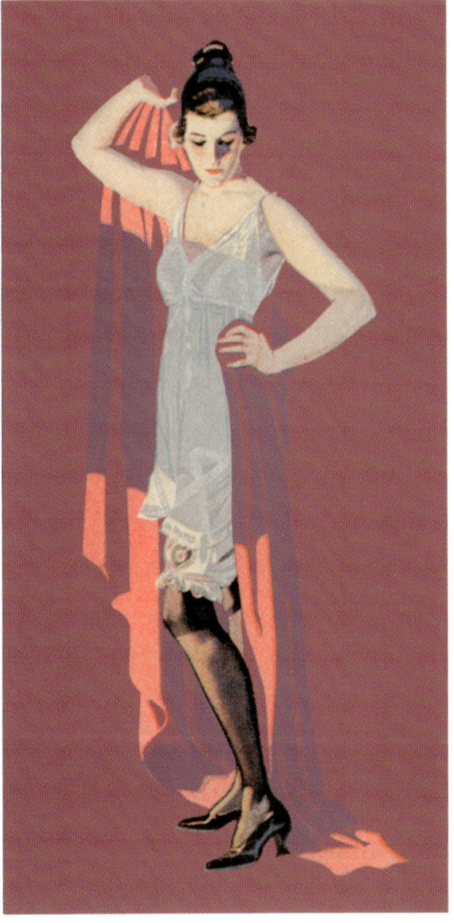

61-64. Ads for Luxite Hosiery.

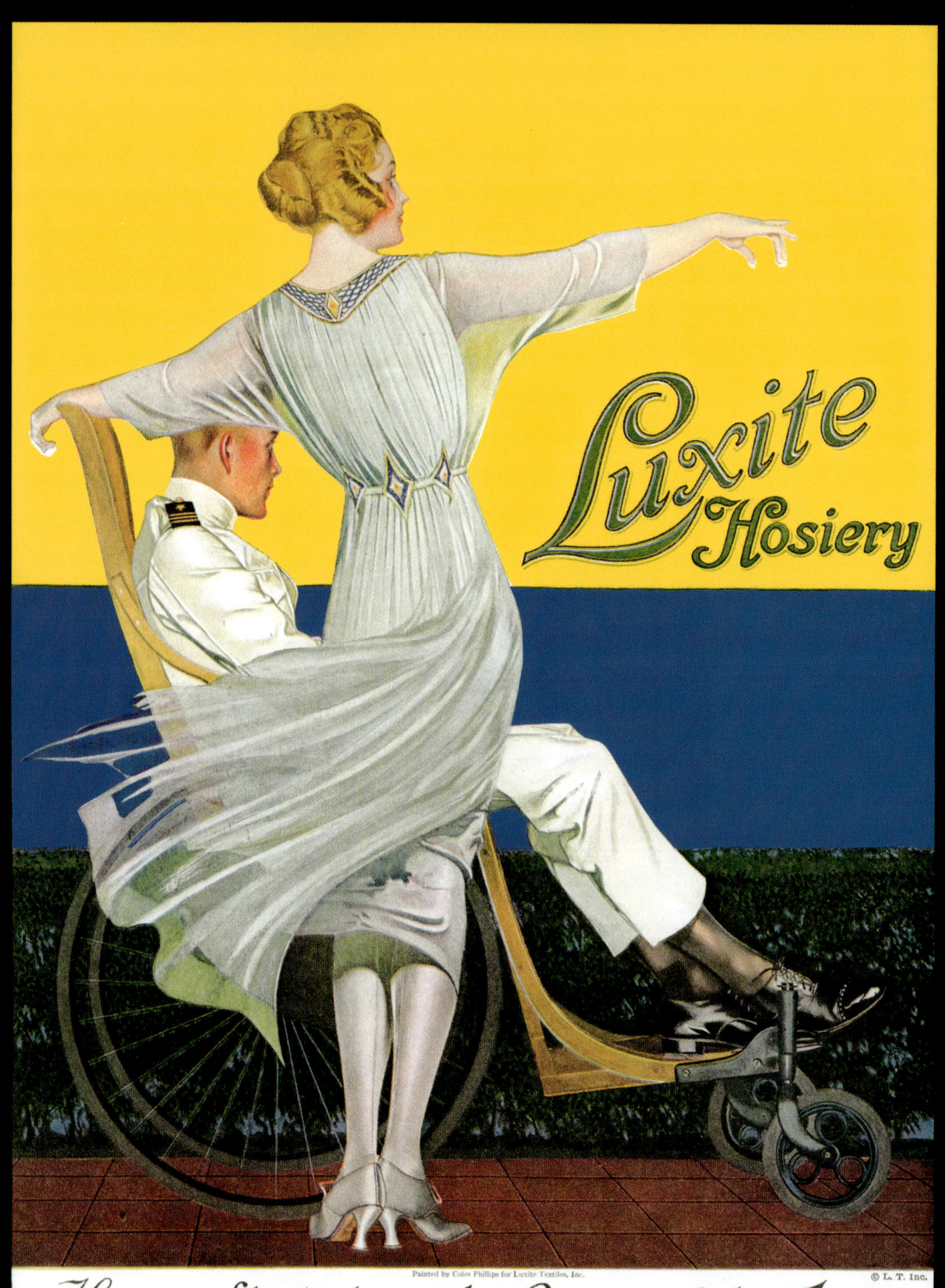

Painted by Coles Phillips for Luxite Textiles, Inc.

© L. T. Inc.

Hose as Shapely as the Curves of the Figure

THE translucent shimmer of Luxite Hosiery half reveals and half conceals. Its texture is so wonderfully soft and silken you can draw a Luxite silk stocking through your finger ring. Luxite launders beautifully because these hose contain no adulterations whatever—nothing but super-fine materials and pure dyes. Naturally Luxite Hosiery wears long and always looks beautiful.

Women's Silk Faced, $1.10; Pure Thread Japanese Silk, $1.30 to $2.25. Other styles 55c upward.
Men's Silk Faced, 65c; Pure Thread Japanese Silk, 85c and $1.10. Other styles 35c up. Children's, 55c up.

LUXITE TEXTILES, Inc., 654 Fowler Street, Milwaukee, Wisconsin

New York Chicago San Francisco *Makers of High Grade Hosiery Since 1875* Liverpool, England Sydney, Australia

LUXITE TEXTILES OF CANADA, Limited, London, Ont.

(984)

COLES PHILLIPS

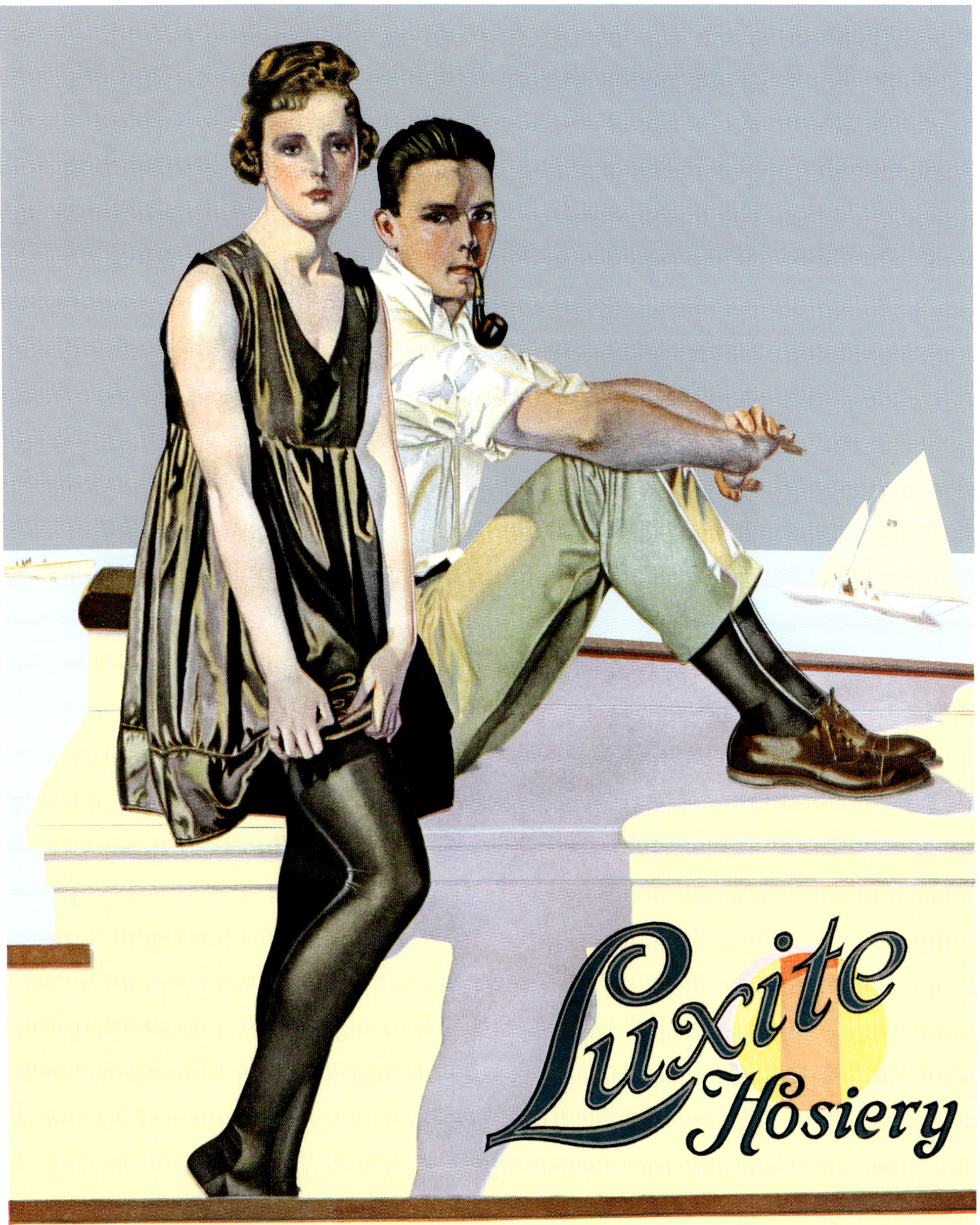
Luxite
Hosiery
COLES PHILLIPS

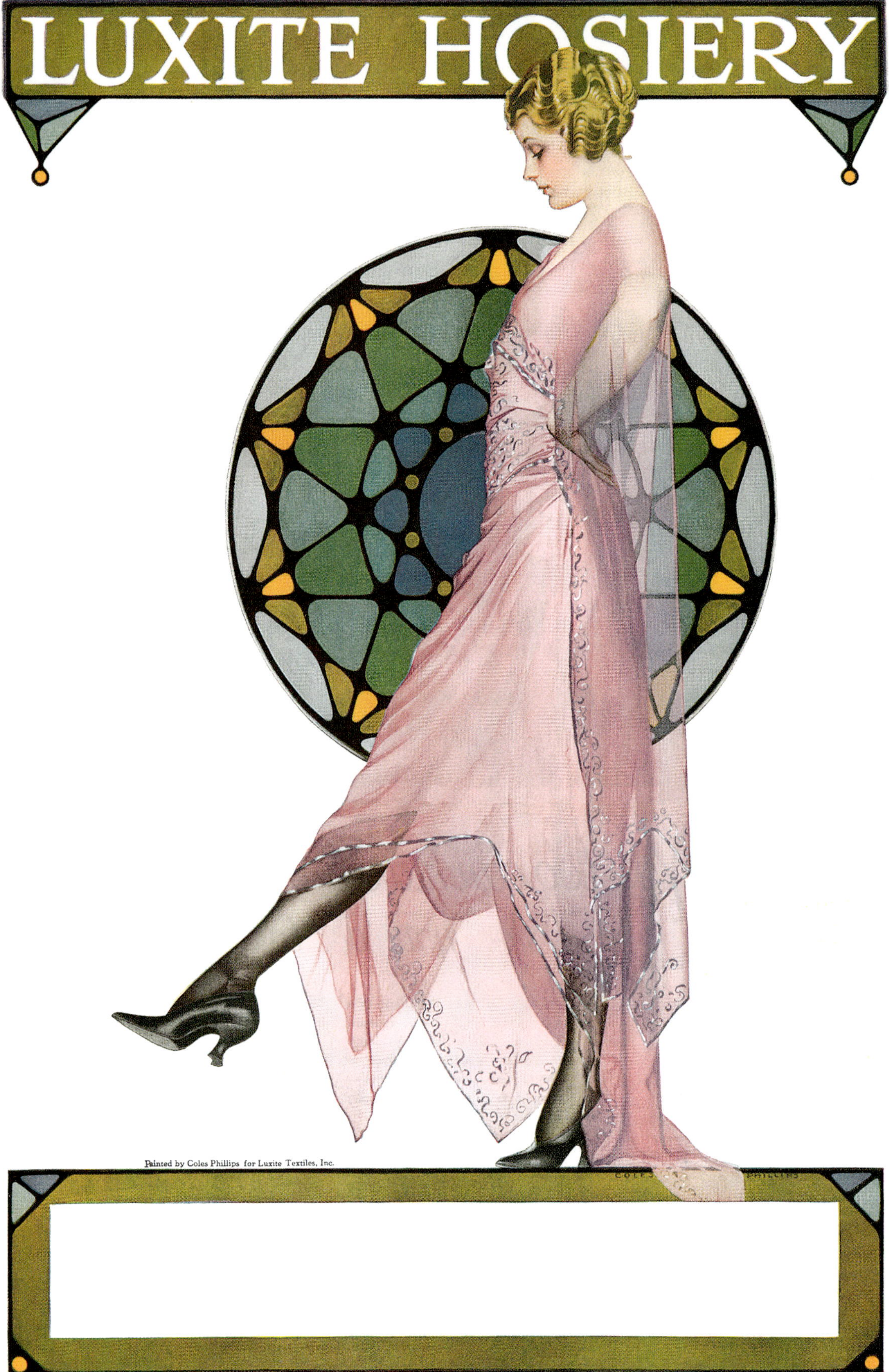
LUXITE HOSIERY
Painted by Coles Phillips for Luxite Textiles, Inc.

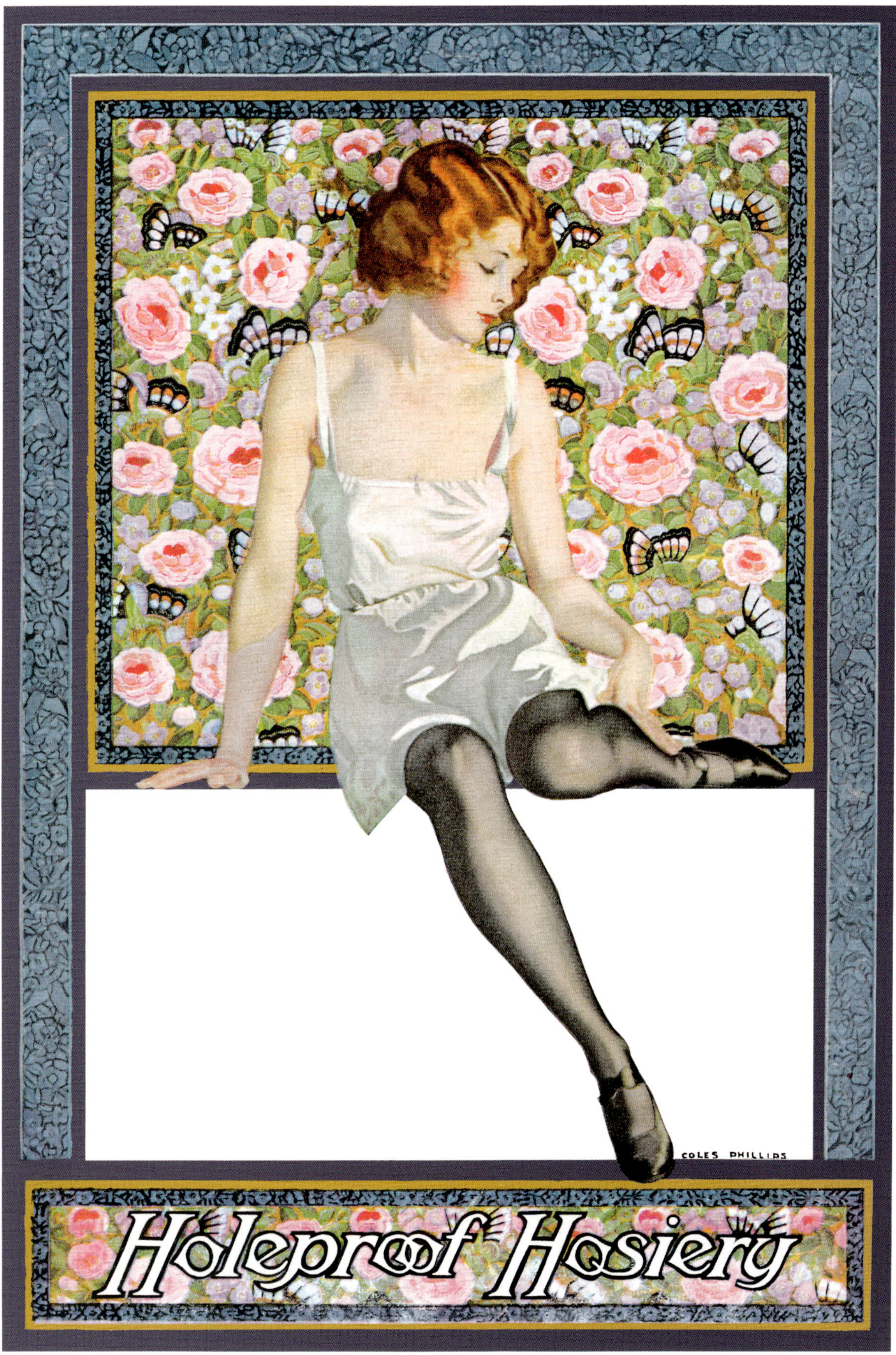

65-69. Ads for Holeproof Hosiery

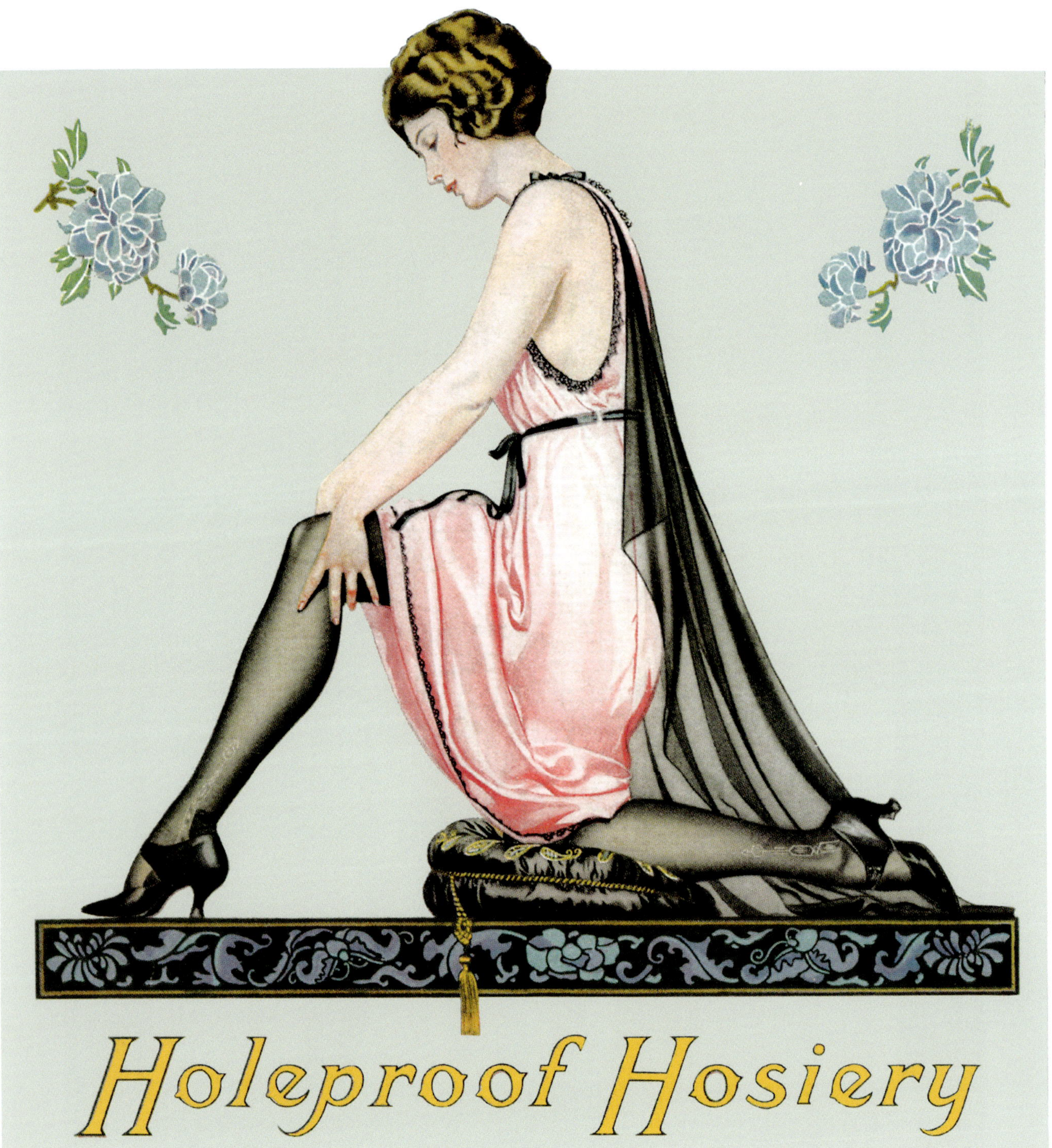
Holeproof Hosiery

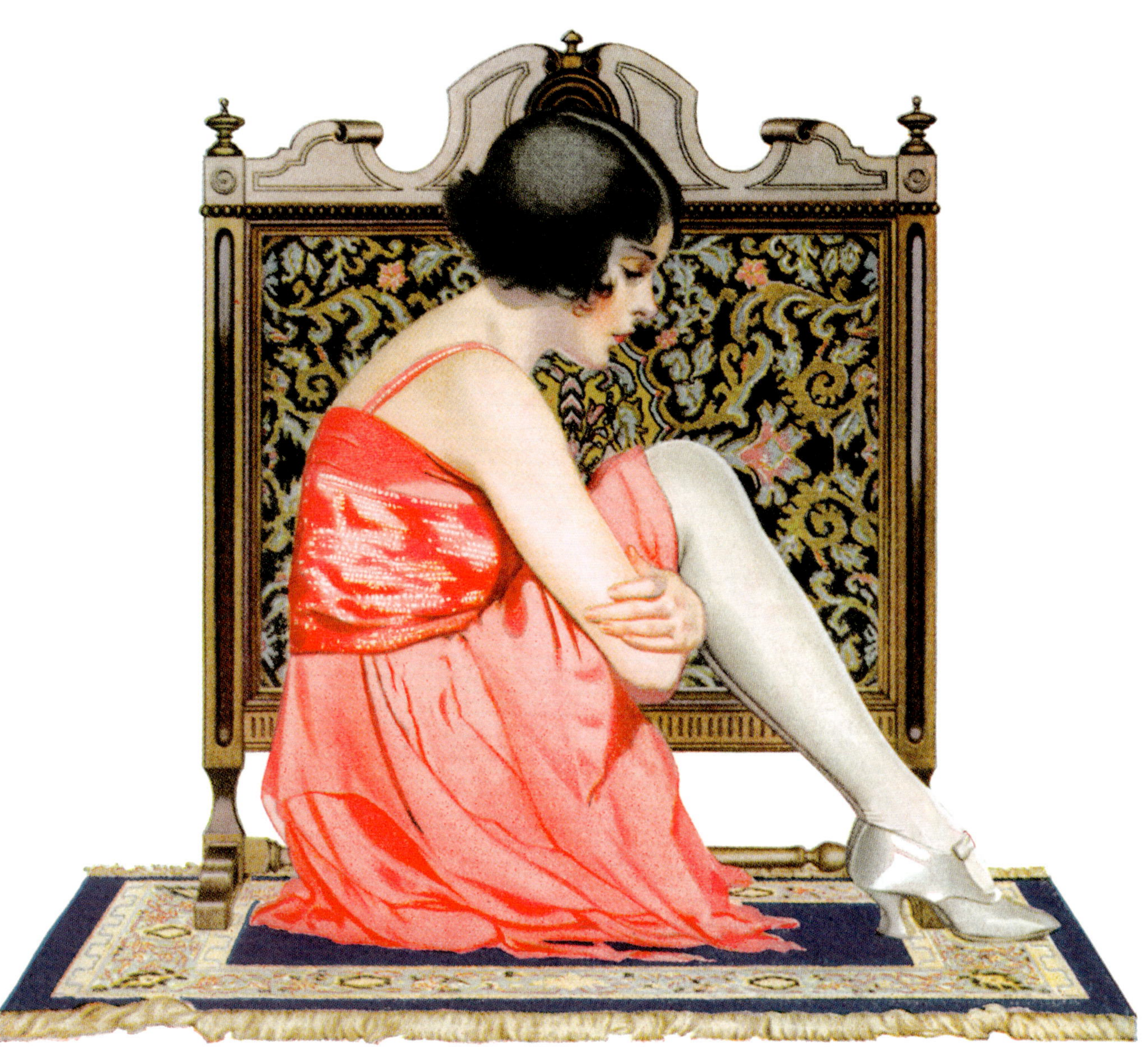

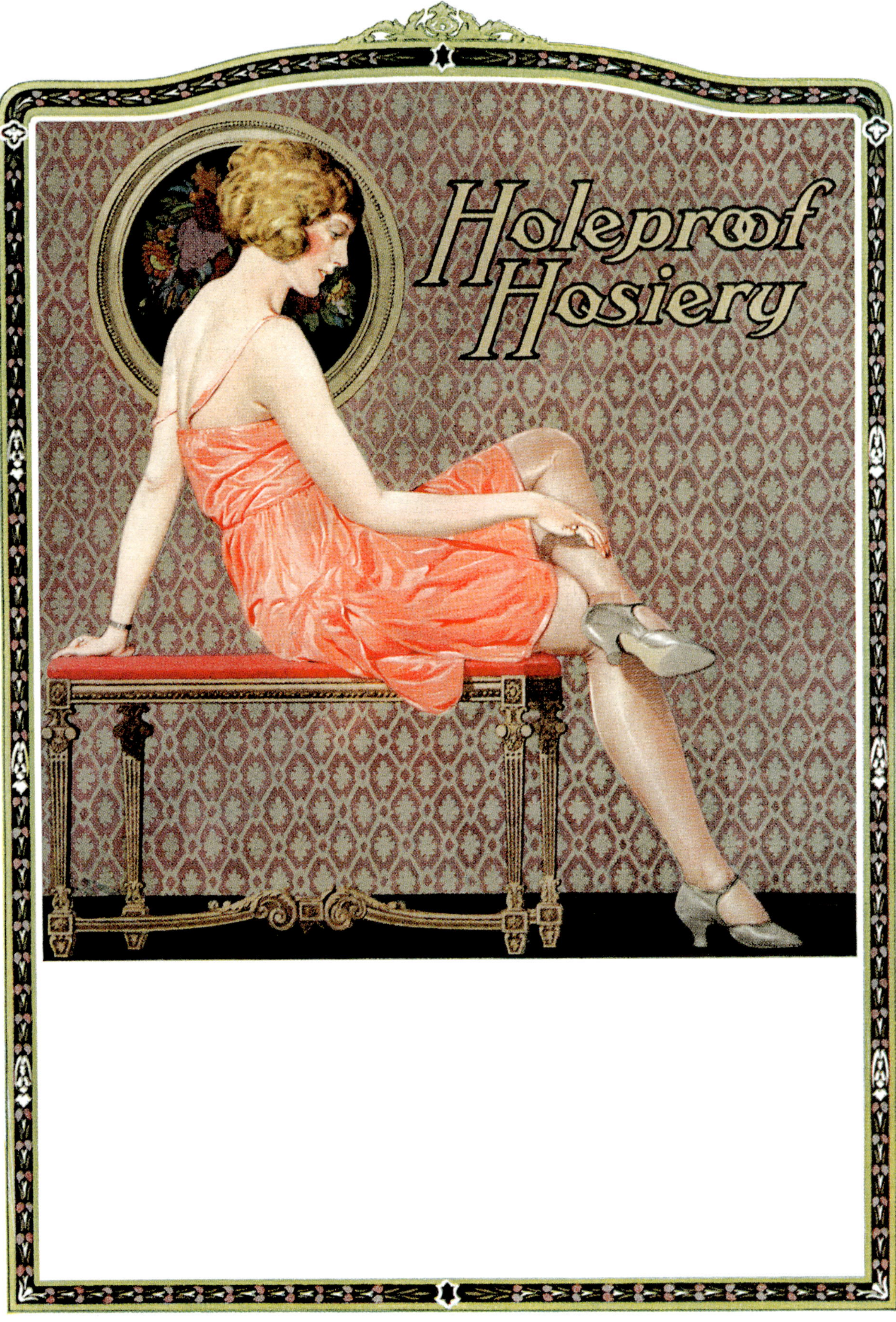
Holeproof
Hosiery

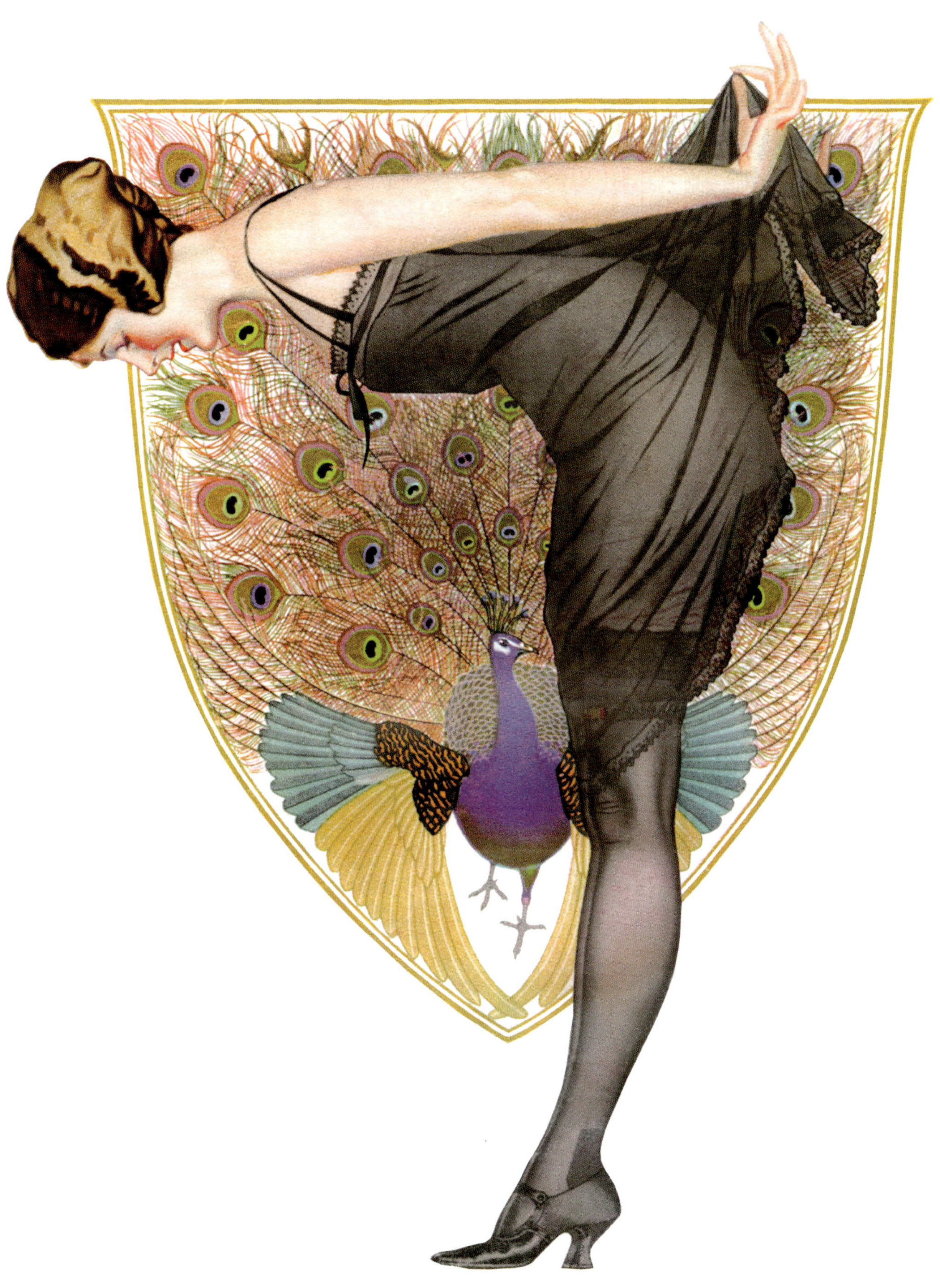

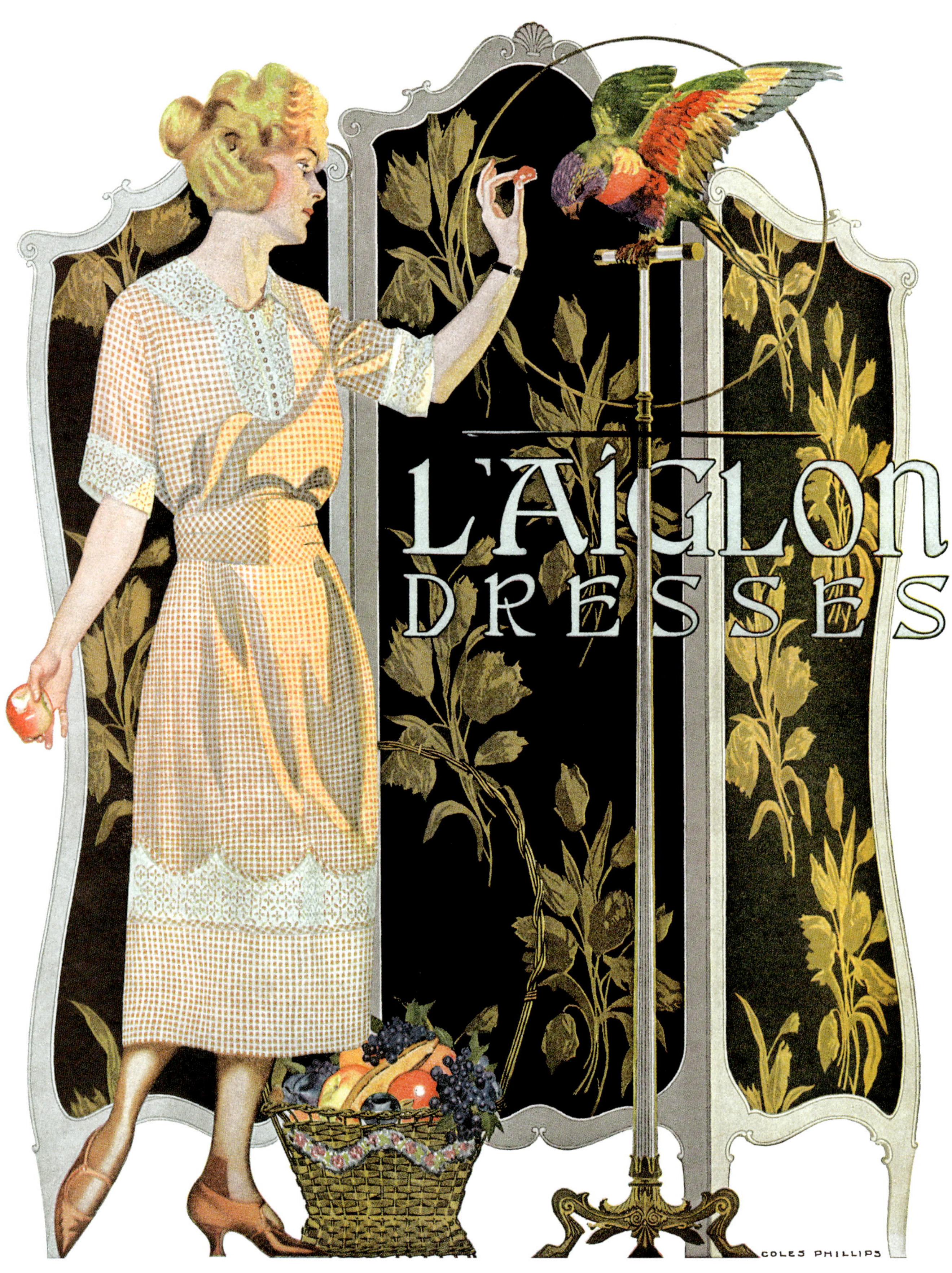

70. L'Aiglon Dress ad, 1921

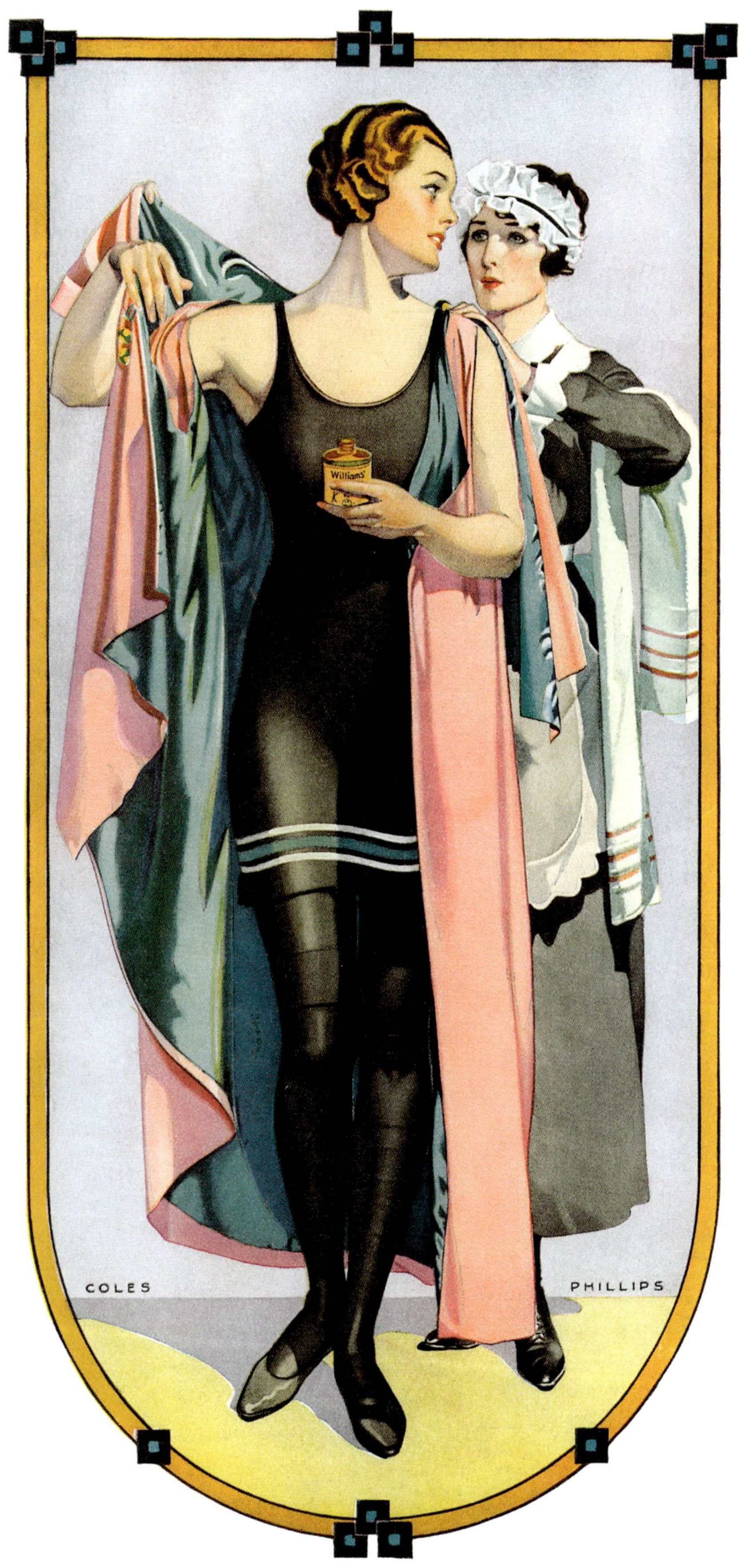

71. Williams' Talc Powder ad, 1919

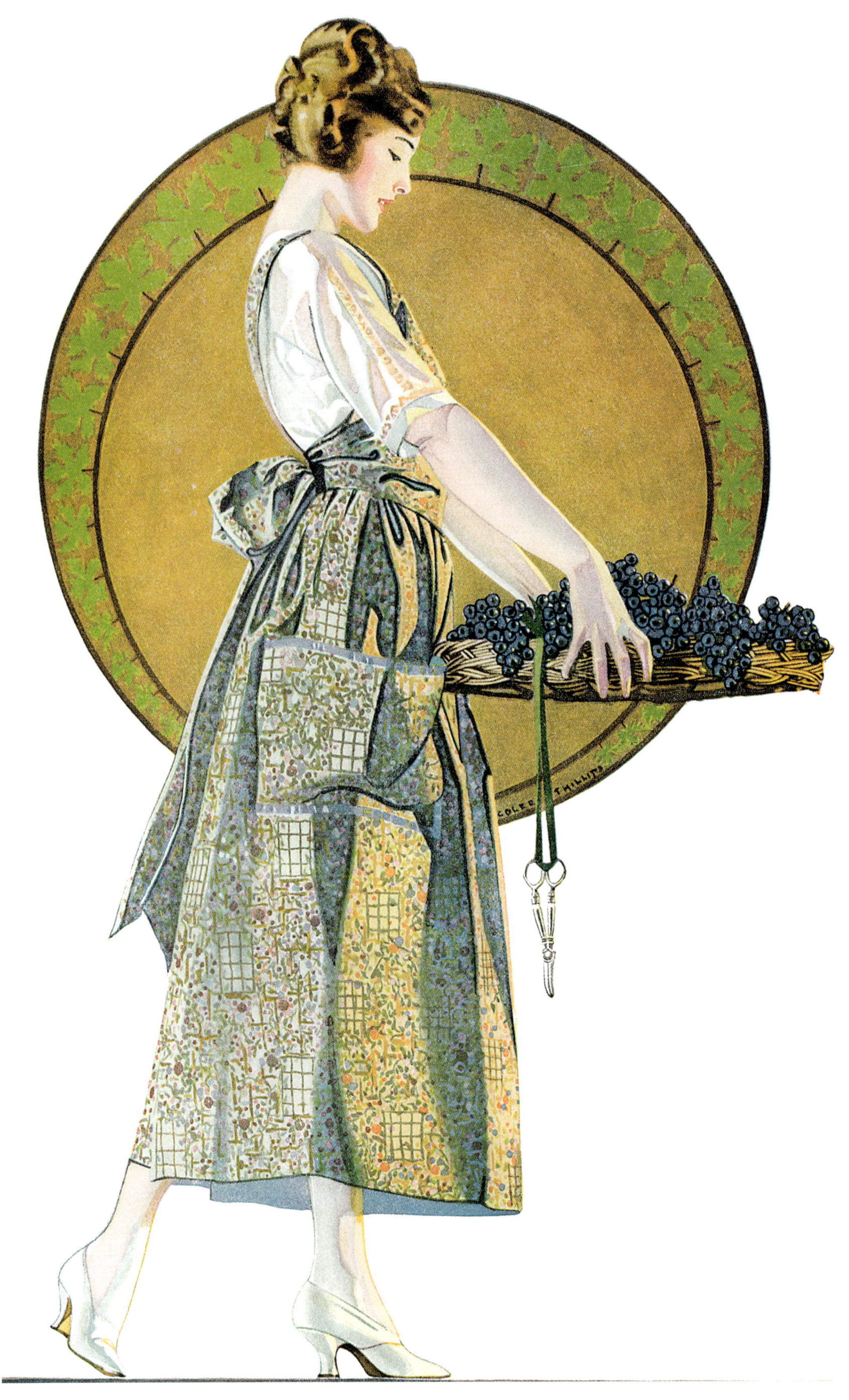

72. Adams Gum ad, 1920

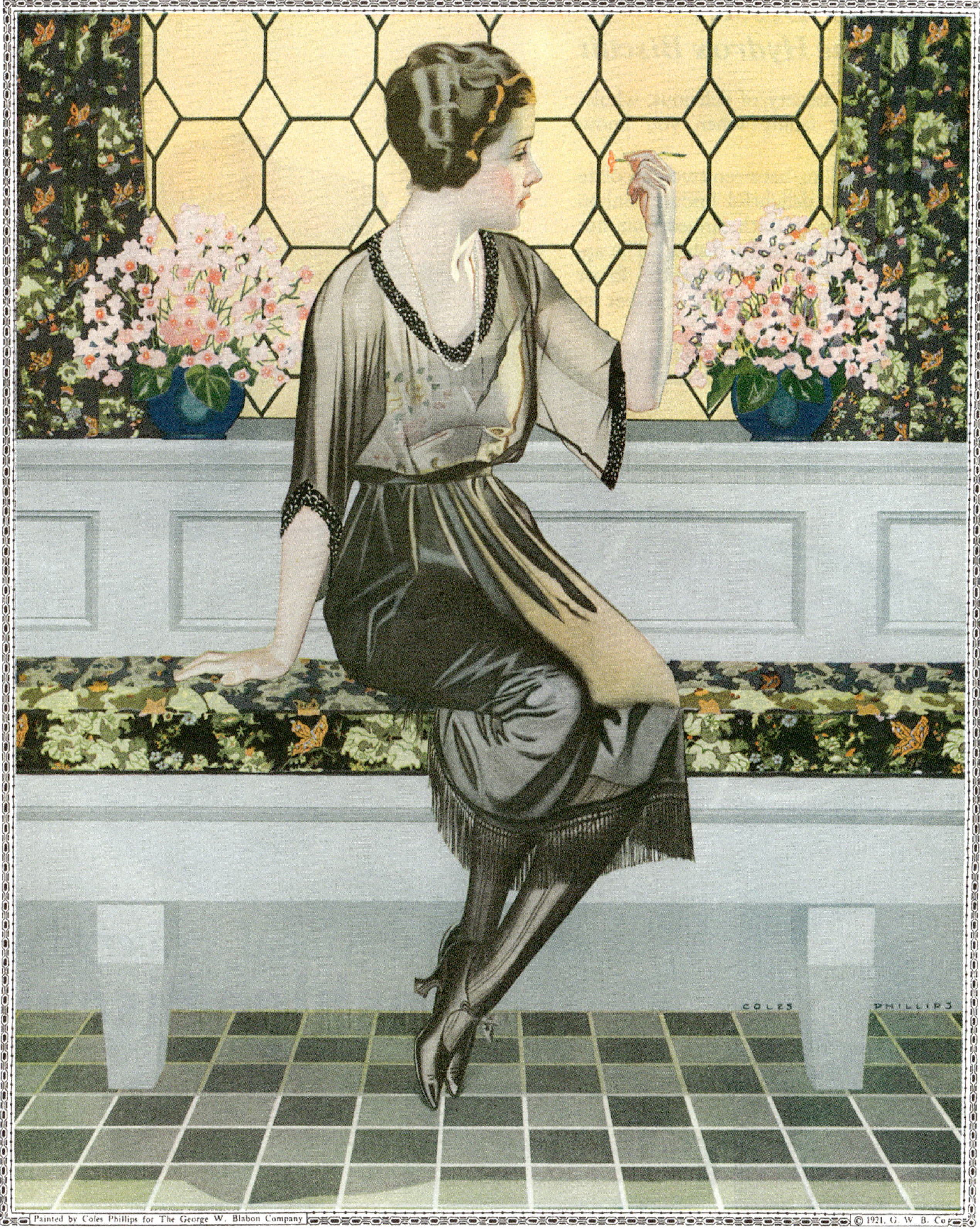

73. Blabon Linoleum ad, 1921

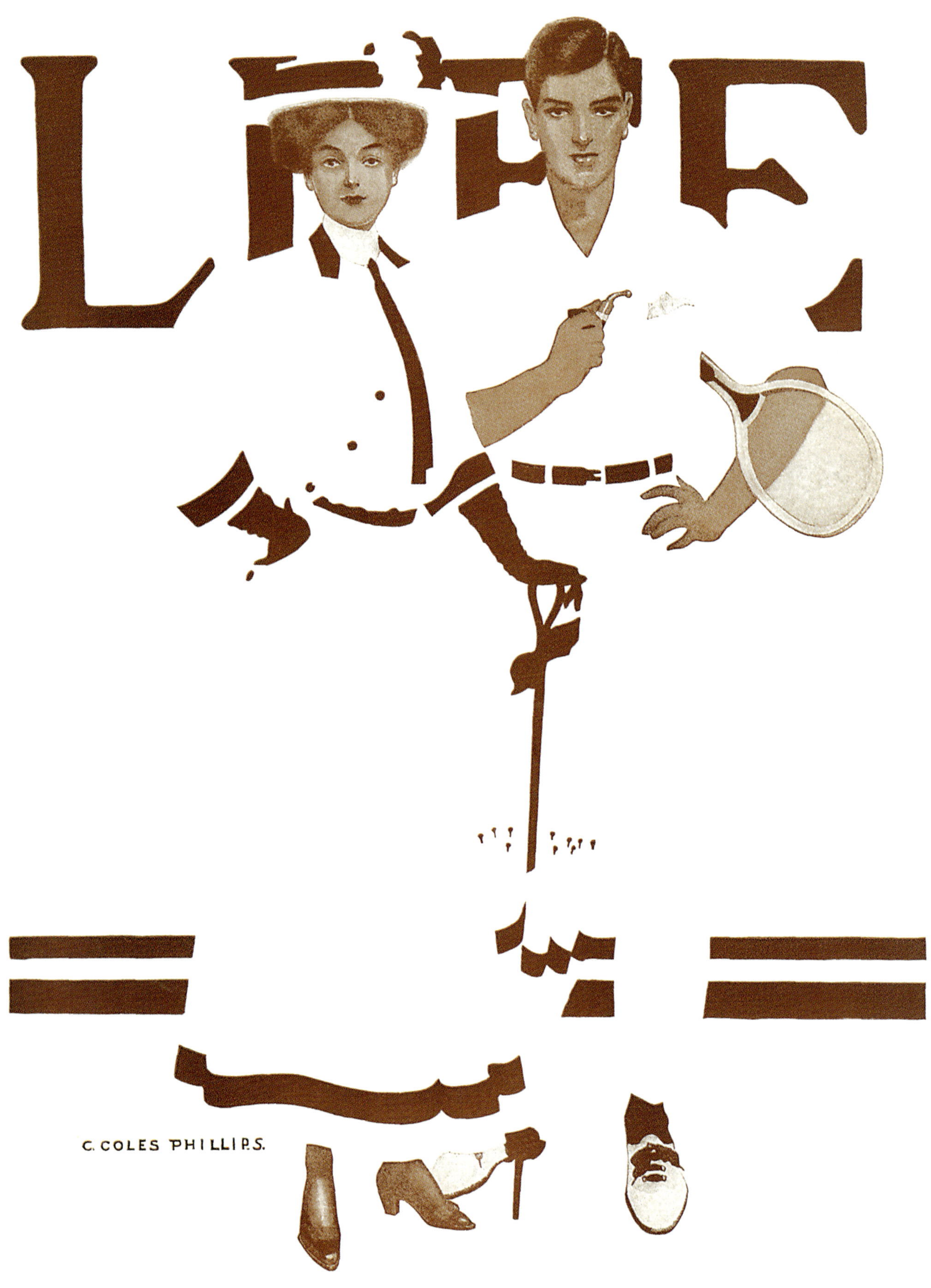

74. *Match, Set*
Cover art from *Life* Magazine, July 9, 1908

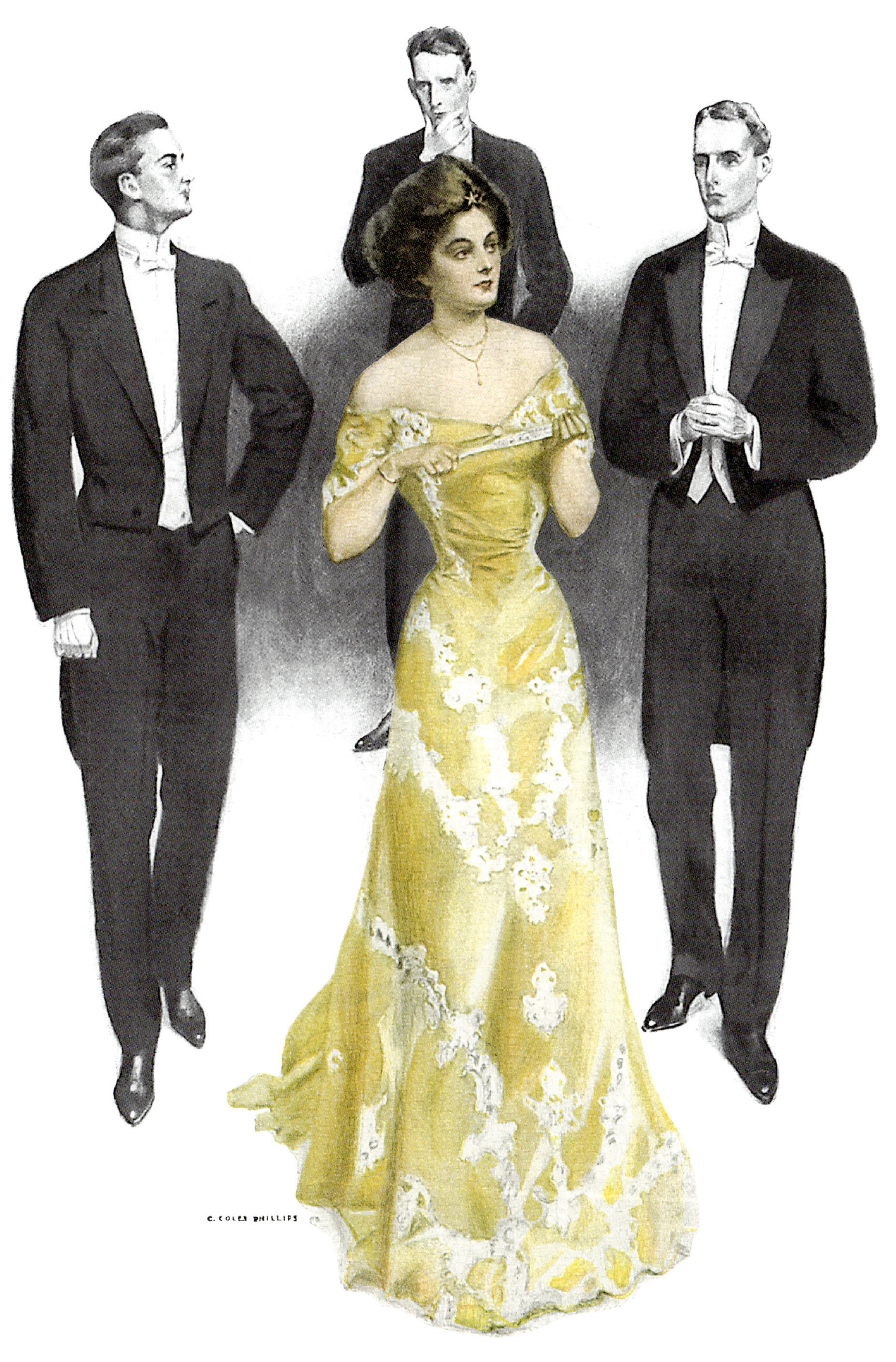

75. *The Three Wise Men*
Cover art from *Life* Magazine, December 3, 1908

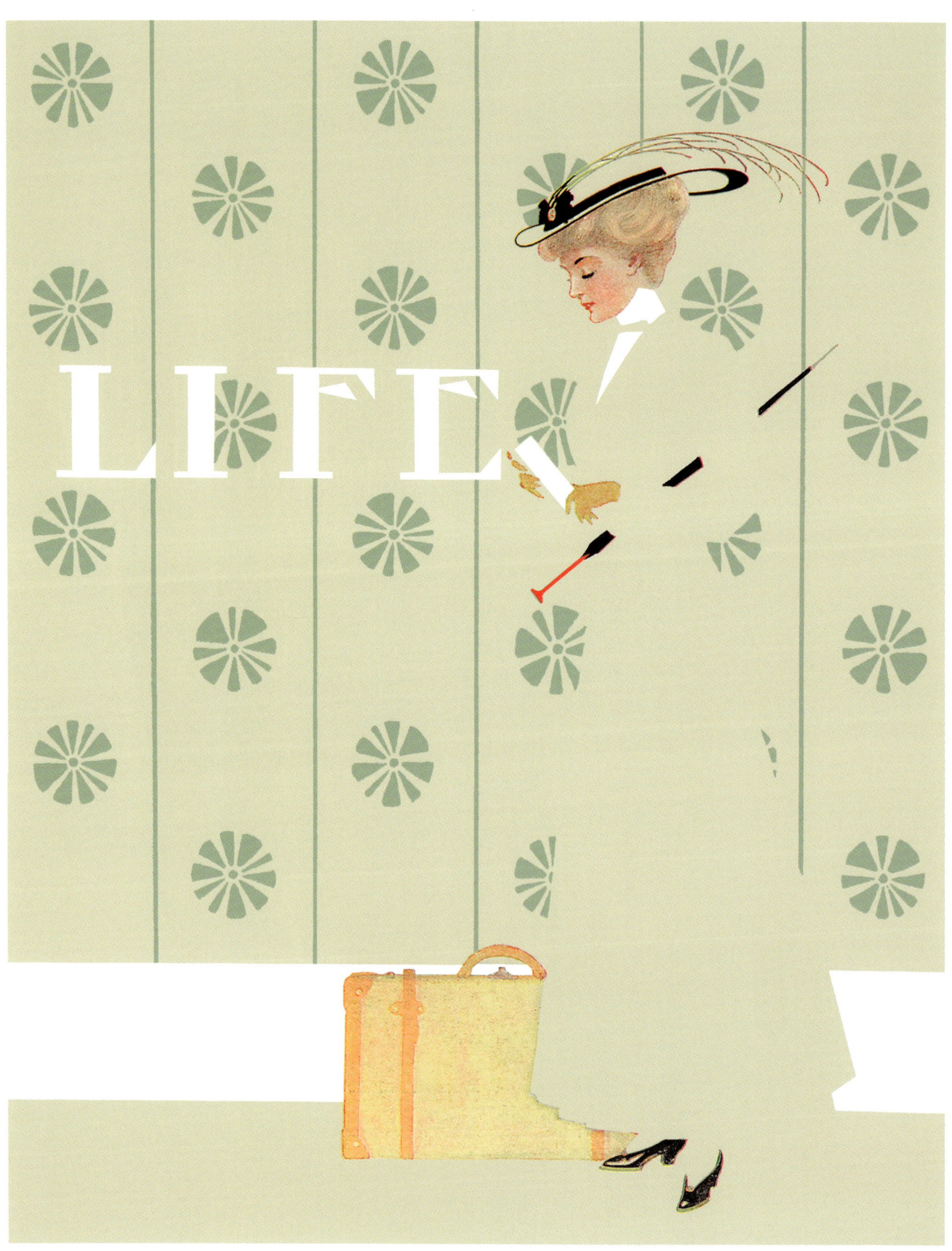

76. *Travel Plans*
Cover art from *Life* Magazine, September 17, 1908

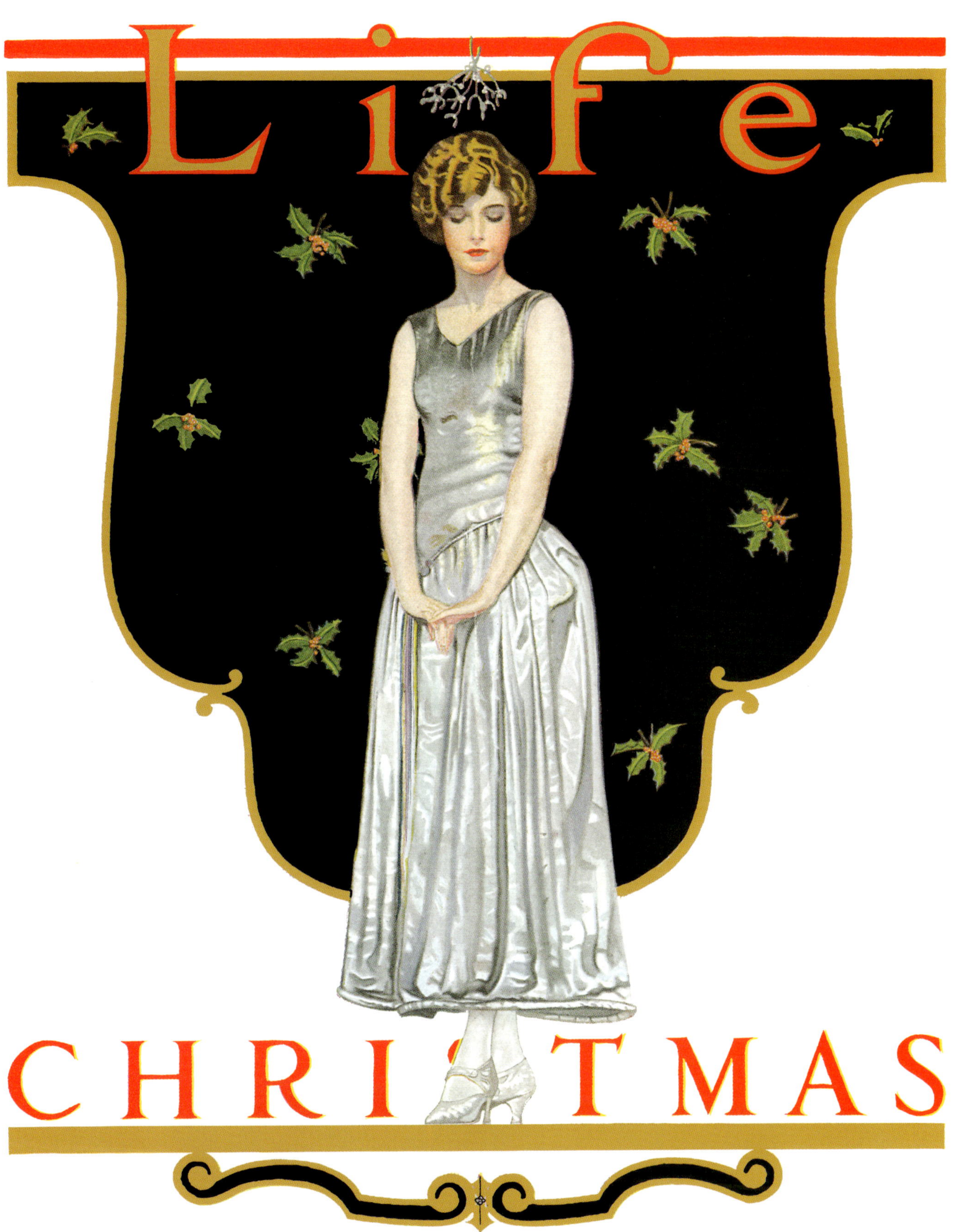

77. *A Lady in Waiting*
Cover art from *Life* Magazine, December 6, 1923

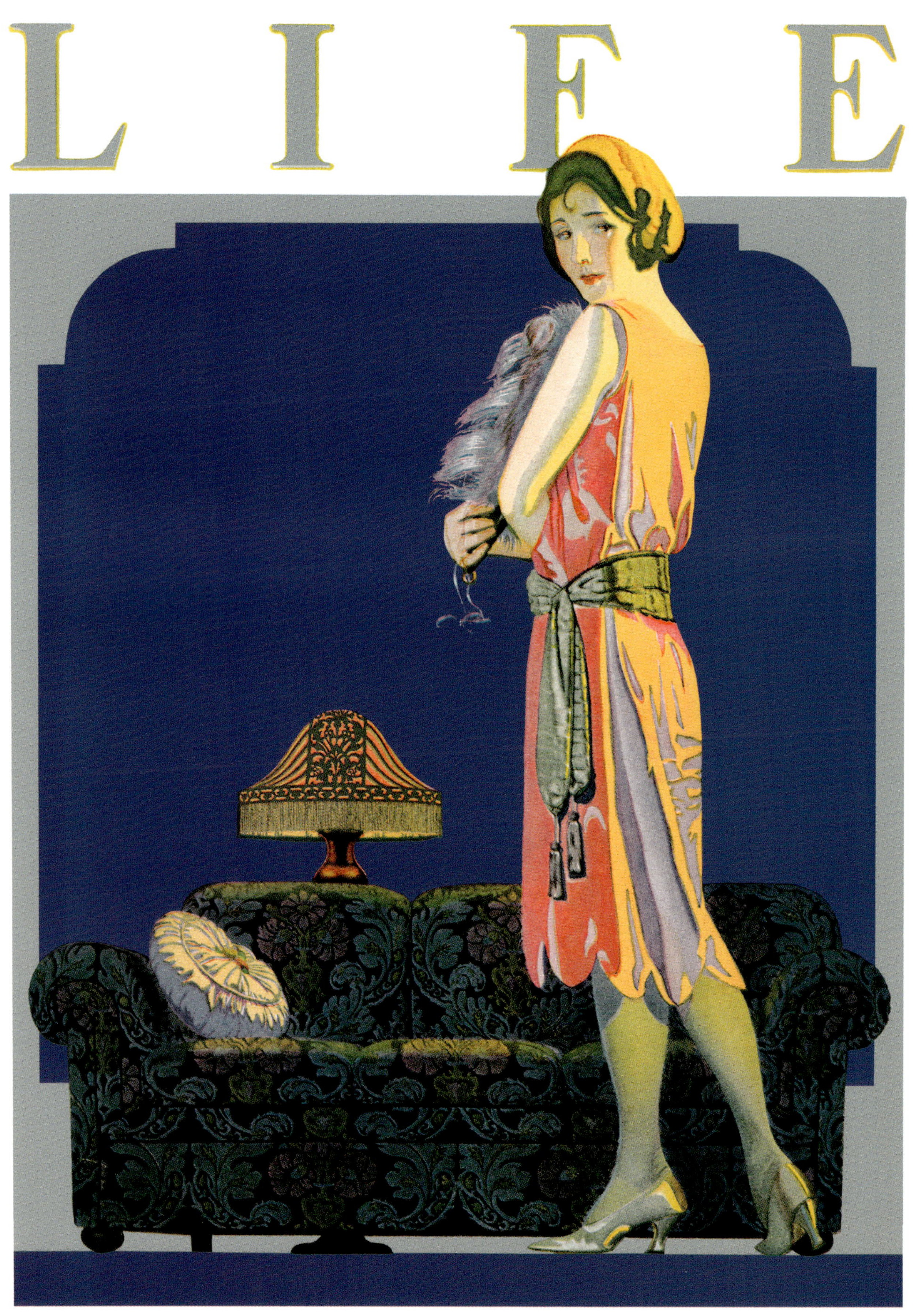

78. *The Leading Lady*
Cover art from *Life* Magazine, May 4, 1922

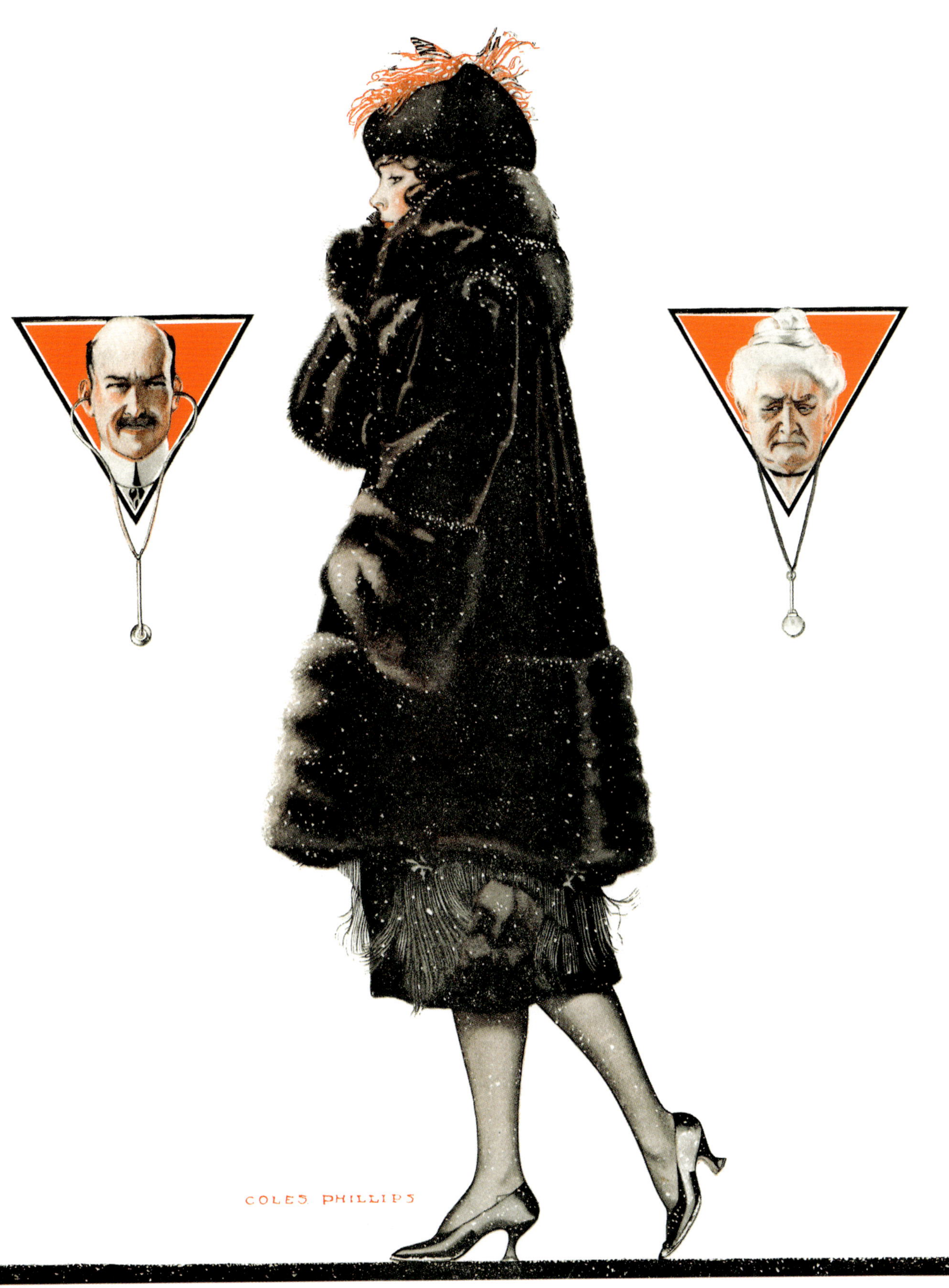

79. Cover art from *The Saturday Evening Post* Magazine
January 22, 1922

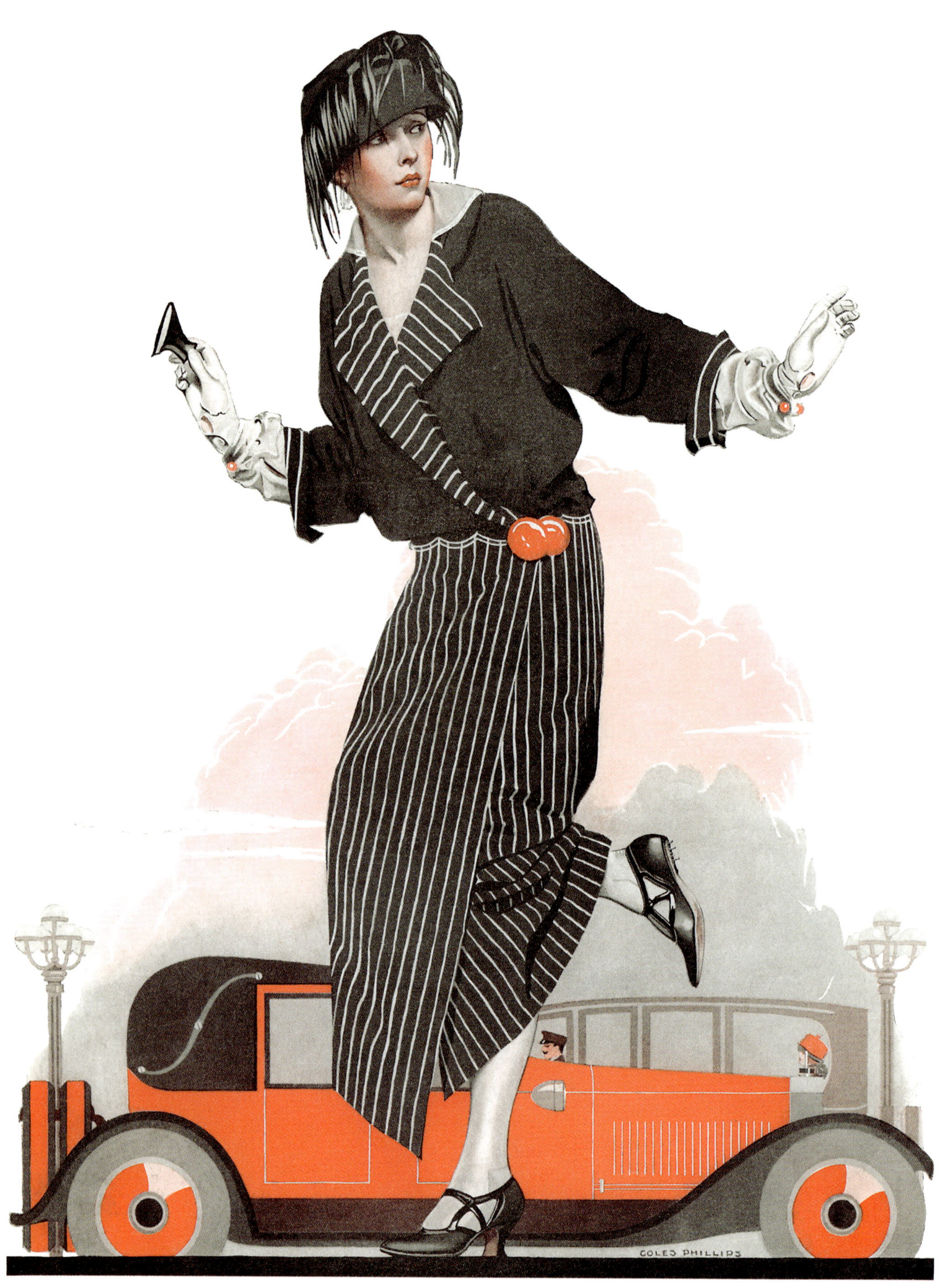

80. Cover art from *The Saturday Evening Post* Magazine
September 23, 1922

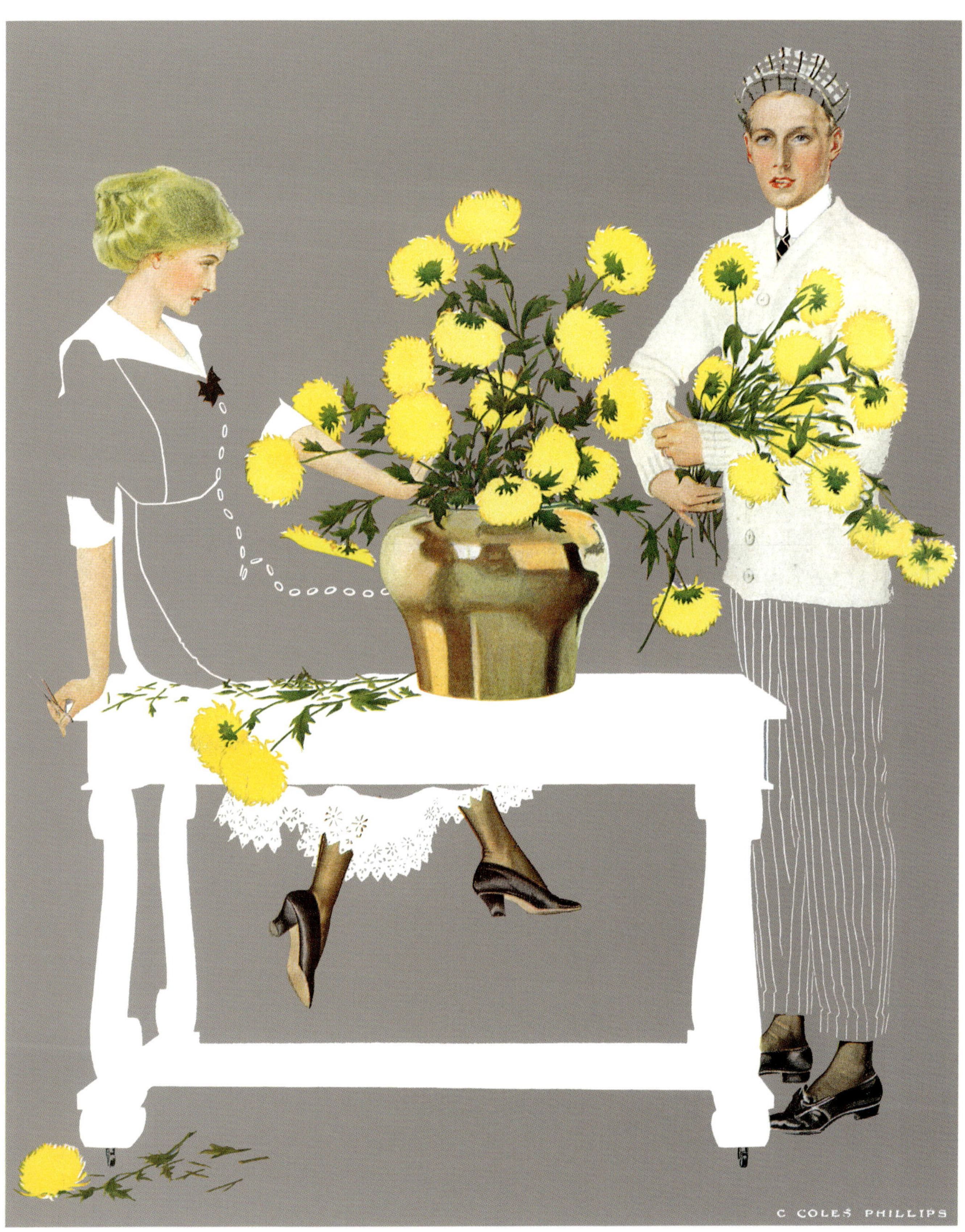

81. Cover art from *The Ladies' Home Journal*
November 1911

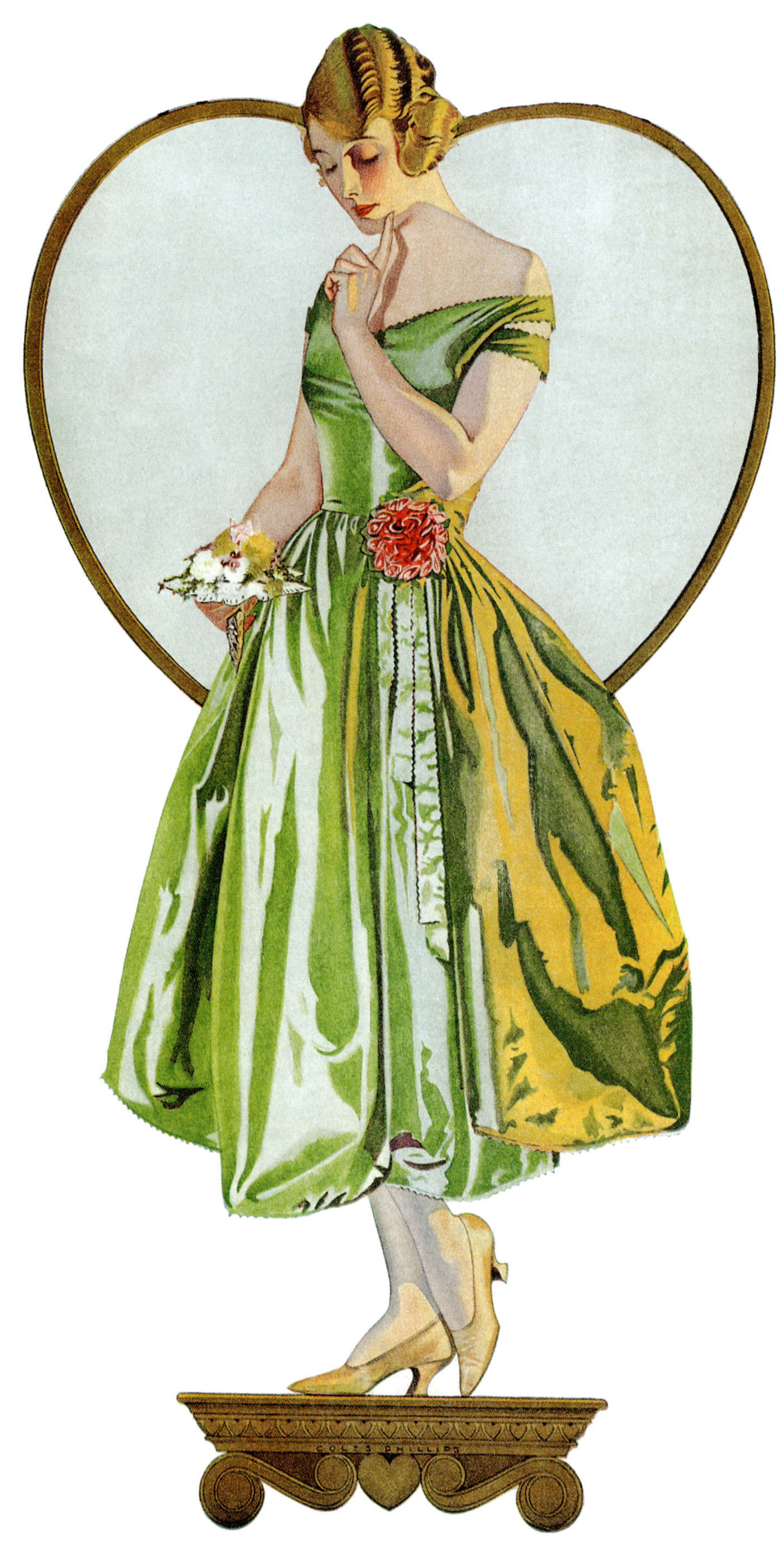

82. Cover art from *The Ladies' Home Journal*
February 1921

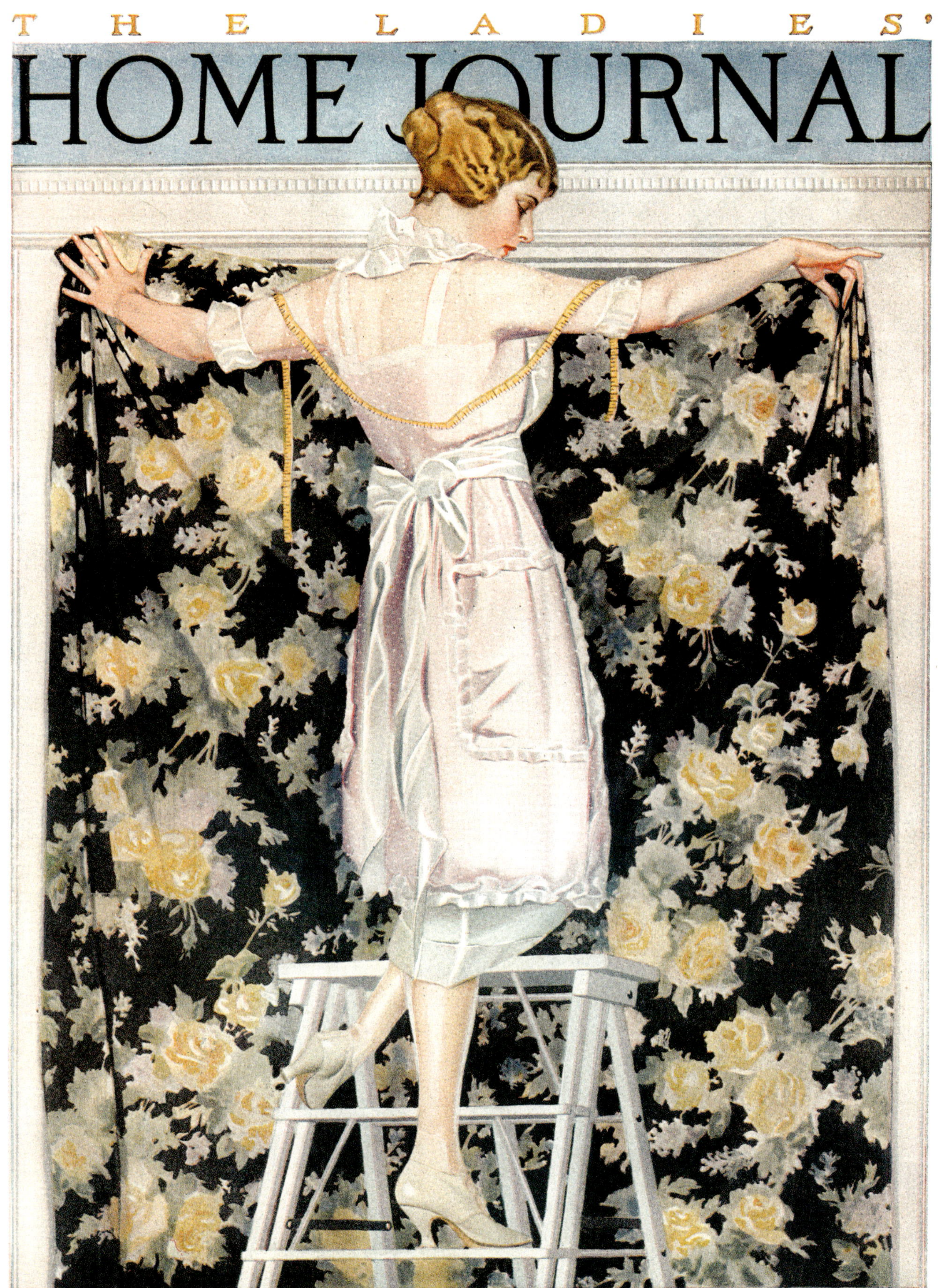

83. Cover art from *The Ladies' Home Journal*
October 1921

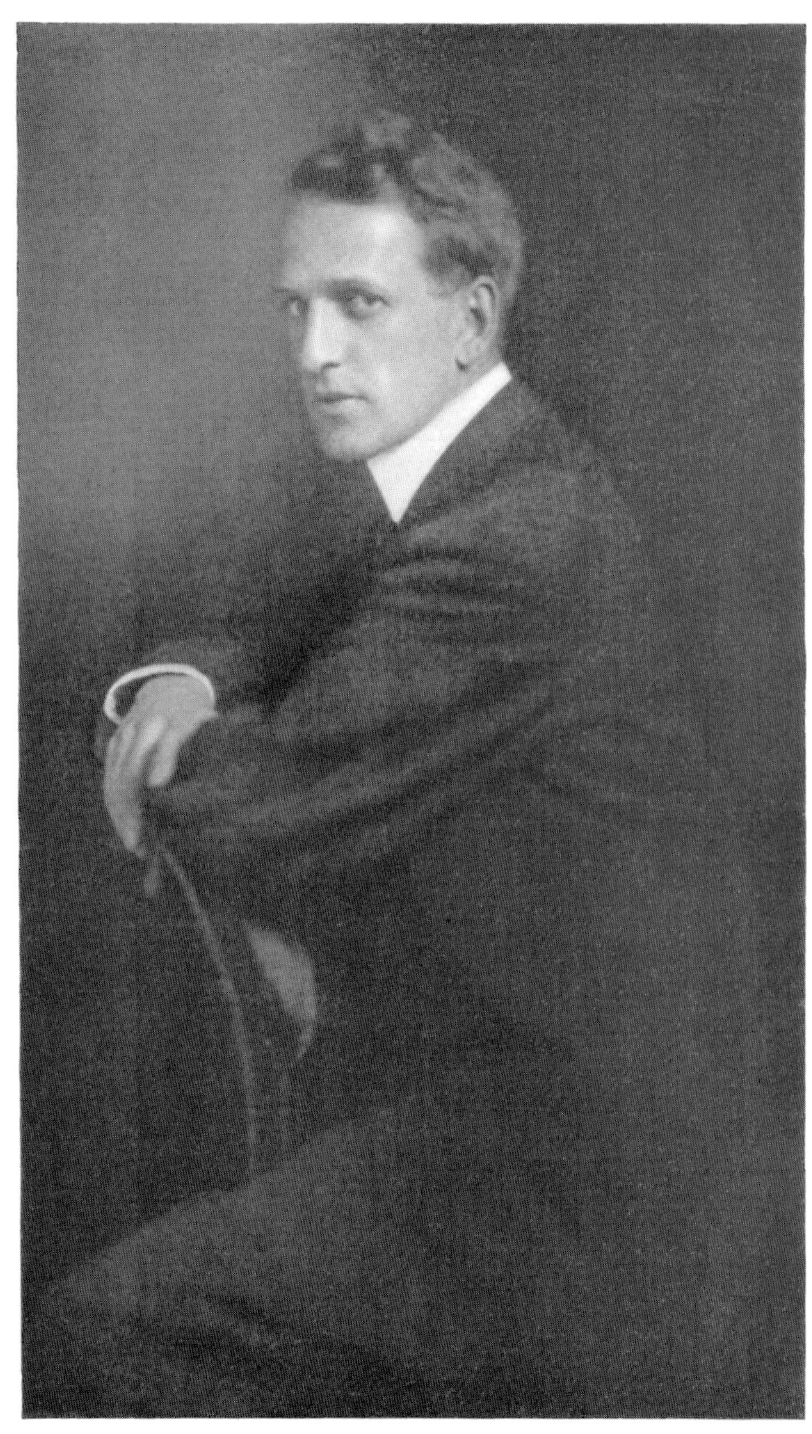

COLES PHILLIPS

Coles Phillips and his Work

The creator of the Fadeaway Girl was born in Springfield, Ohio, thirty-one years ago. There was little of the artistic temperament in his early years, rather more of the healthy, fun-loving boy's capacity to fall into deviltry, and it was not until his college days that he realized that his natural ability to draw might be of use to him. In his efforts to work his way through Kenyon College at Gambier, Ohio, he earned his first money as an artist by illustrating and decorating the college monthly magazine. After his graduation at the age of twenty-one, he went to New York and for some time picked up a varied experience here and there, clerking and working at odd jobs. Later he found employment as a solicitor in one of the city's biggest advertising and designing houses. In this position he represented his chosen field and cultivated a keen business sense and a practical knowledge of commercial art.

He soon used this knowledge to good advantage in forming a dozen artists into an advertising organization of his own. In this new adventure he was forced to spend so much time as "outside man" on the business end of the concern that his painting suffered from neglect. But he finally responded to the call of the artist in him, retired from the commercial field, rented a studio, and set out to remedy his lack of technical training by attending the Chase School in the afternoons and the Free Art School on Forty-fourth street in the evenings.

On his first drawing Phillips worked a month. *Life* accepted it as a double-page cartoon and proceeded at once to look up Phillips. He immediately became a regular contributor, and when *Life* issued colored covers the Fadeaway Girl made her bow to lovers of the daintily feminine. Her success was instantaneous, and her type with its elusive lines and its happy blending of colors, has become famous the country over. So original was the conception that the Fadeaway Girl will always stand for Coles Phillips and Coles Phillips for the Fadeaway Girl. He says, however, that his other achievements with the brush have done more to bring him success than the fadeaway drawings.

Admirers of the art of Phillips little realize the amount of work required in these apparently simple creations. So much of the surrounding detail is eliminated that it is doubly imperative to show the central figure to its best advantage. Therefore, since his artistic efforts must be produced with so few actual lines, every drawing demands the most careful study. To do with truth to life, Phillips always uses living models.

The originator of the Fadeaway Girl is not of the long-haired, flowing bow-tie variety of artists, but prides himself on his practicality and enjoys having his friends call him "sane and business-like," which he is. He lives in New Rochelle, the New York suburb which now has another claim to fame than the fact that it is "Forty-five Minutes from Broadway," and there in his studio overlooking Long Island Sound, with his slender, sweet-faced wife as a model, he does much of his best work. For the wife of C. Coles Phillips is the inspiration of the art that has made him famous. America has opened wide her arms to welcome this new creation. The Coles Phillips Girl typifies the subtle charm of American Womanhood. On the drawing-room or in the kitchen, breaking hearts or baking pies, or sturdily joying in the mighty stillness of the great outdoors, always alluring, always at home, a real woman from the tip of her dainty boot to the soft glory of her hair, she stands out from her flat background and answers completely to a young man's fancy at its highest and best.

From *A Young Man's Fancy*, 1912